Happy Birth[day]
Rebecca
love
from Daddy
and Mummy.
xxo

PHILIP'S
CHILDREN'S
▷ATLAS◁

NEW EDITION

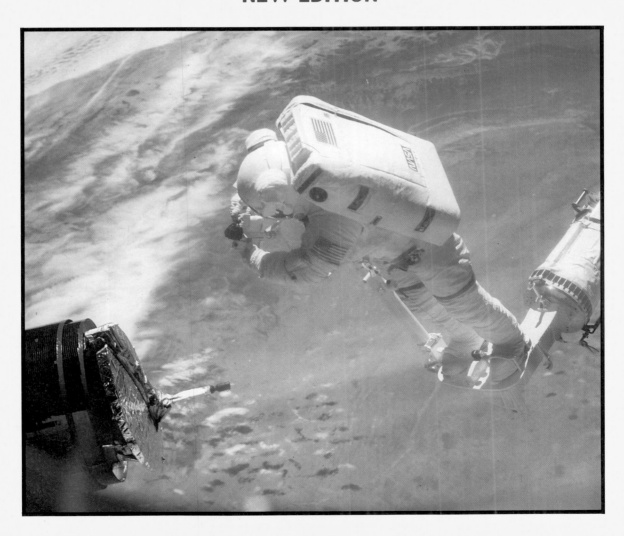

DAVID AND JILL WRIGHT

GEORGE
PHILIP

CONTENTS

To Rachel and Steven

British Library Cataloguing in Publication Data
Wright, David, 1939–
Philip's children's atlas—2nd ed.
1. World. Atlases. For children
I. Title   II. Wright, Jill, 1942–
912
ISBN 0-540-01196-7

Text copyright © 1989 by David and Jill Wright
Maps copyright © 1989 George Philip Ltd

First edition 1987
Second edition 1989
Reprinted 1990

Printed in Hong Kong

Cover photographs

Front cover. Top right: Fruit seller in Peru. *Paul Snow*. Bottom right: Door painting in Katmandu, Nepal. *Jude Welton*. Bottom left: Junk and skyscrapers, Hong Kong harbour. *R. Ian Lloyd/The Hutchison Library*. Centre: Apollo astronaut's view of the Earth. NASA.

Back cover. Children in Patan, Nepal, in front of a shrine to the elephant-headed god, Ganesh. *Jude Welton*.

OUR PLANET EARTH

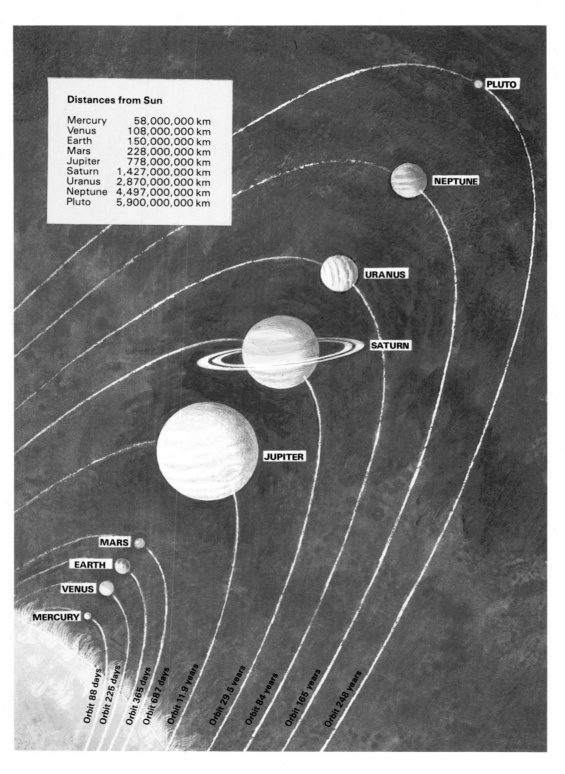

Distances from Sun

Mercury	58,000,000 km
Venus	108,000,000 km
Earth	150,000,000 km
Mars	228,000,000 km
Jupiter	778,000,000 km
Saturn	1,427,000,000 km
Uranus	2,870,000,000 km
Neptune	4,497,000,000 km
Pluto	5,900,000,000 km

PLUTO

NEPTUNE

URANUS

SATURN

JUPITER

MARS

EARTH

VENUS

MERCURY

Orbit 88 days
Orbit 225 days
Orbit 365 days
Orbit 687 days
Orbit 11.9 years
Orbit 29.5 years
Orbit 84 years
Orbit 165 years
Orbit 248 years

Our planet Earth is one of nine planets that travel round the Sun. The diagram (*left*) shows that we are 150 million kilometres away from the Sun. It takes $365\frac{1}{4}$ days for the Earth to travel all the way round the Sun – which we call a year. Every four years we add an extra day to February to use up the $\frac{1}{4}$ days. This is called a Leap Year. The Earth travels at a speed of more than 107,000 kilometres an hour. (In fact, you have travelled 600 kilometres through space while reading this far!)

As the Earth travels through space, it is also spinning round and round. It spins round once in 24 hours, which we call a day. Places on the Equator are spinning at 1660 kilometres an hour. Because of the way the Earth spins, we experience day and night, and different seasons during a year (see page 13). No part of our planet is too hot or too cold for life to survive.

Our nearest neighbour in space is the Moon – 384,400 kilometres away. The first men to reach the Moon took four days to travel there in 1969. On the way, they took photographs of the Earth, such as the one on the right. The Earth looks very blue from space because of all the sea. It is the only planet in the Solar System with sea. Look at the swirls of cloud, especially over southern Africa and over northern Europe. These show that the Earth has an atmosphere. Our atmosphere contains oxygen and water vapour and it keeps us and all other living things alive. We could not breathe on any other planet.

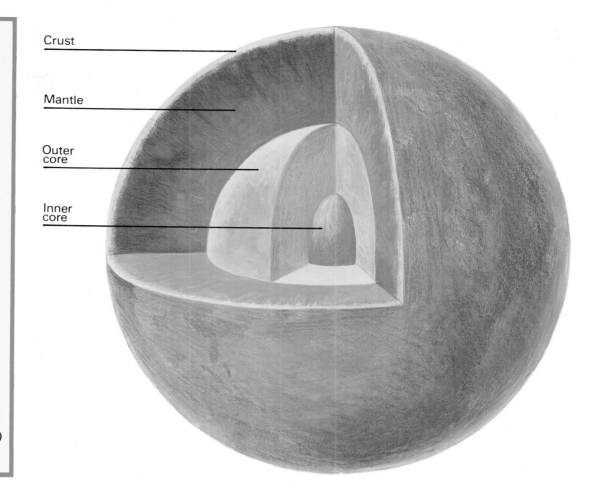

Crust

Mantle

Outer
core

Inner
core

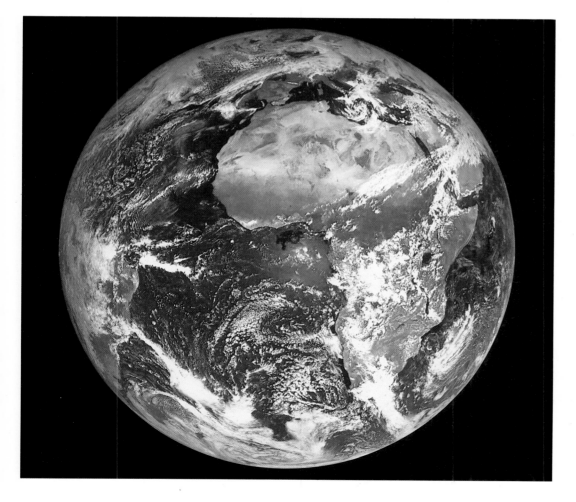

Scientists believe that our Earth is made of layers of rock. The diagram above shows the Earth with a slice cut out. The hottest part is the core, at the centre. Around the core is the mantle. The outer layer, the crust, is very thin under the oceans, but it is thicker under the continents. Scientists now know that the Earth's crust is cracked, like the shell of a hard-boiled egg that has been dropped. The cracks are called faults. The huge sections of crust divided by the faults are called plates and they are moving very, very slowly. Over millions and millions of years, the continents have gradually moved across the Earth's surface as the crustal plates have moved. Sudden movements near the faults cause earthquakes or volcanic eruptions. The satellite photo (*left*) shows all of Africa and a small part of South America. These two continents were once joined together, but about 100 million years ago they began to split apart.

MOUNTAINS, PLAINS AND SEAS

The map shows that there is much more sea than land in the world. The Pacific is by far the biggest ocean; the map splits it in two.

Mountains are shown in relief on this map. Look for the world's highest mountain range – the Himalayas, in Asia. There are high mountains on the western side of both American continents. Most of the world's great mountain ranges have been made by folding in the Earth's crust.

Desert areas are in orange. The green expanse across northern Europe and northern Asia is the world's biggest plain.

Part of the Great Plains of North America. *The land is flat as far as the eye can see, but it is also 1000 metres above sea-level – plains are not always lowland.*

Greenland

Rocky Mountains

Great Plains

North America

Grand Canyon

Mississippi

ATLANTIC OCEAN

PACIFIC OCEAN

Angel Falls

Amazon

Andes

South America

Scale along the equator 1:116 000 000

| 0 | 1000km | 2000km | 3000km | 4000km | 5000km |

1cm on the map = 1160 kilometres on the ground

| 0 | 1000 miles | 2000 miles | 3000 miles |

1inch on the map = 1860 miles on the ground

180°

180°

Fact box

Highest mountain Mount Everest, 8848 metres (Asia)
Longest mountain range Andes, 7200 kilometres (S. America)
Longest rivers Nile, 6670 kilometres (Africa); Amazon, 6448 kilometres (S. America)

Longest gorge Grand Canyon, 349 kilometres (N. America)
Highest waterfall Angel Falls, 979 metres (Venezuela, S. America)
Largest lake Caspian Sea, 360,700 square kilometres (but it is shrinking!) (USSR and Iran, Asia)
Deepest lake Lake Baikal, 1940 metres (USSR)

Largest ocean Pacific, 181,000,000 square kilometres
Deepest part of oceans Mariana Trench, 11,022 metres (Pacific)
Largest islands Australia, 7,686,848 square kilometres; Greenland, 2,175,600 square kilometres
Largest desert Sahara, 8,400,000 square kilometres (Africa)

COUNTRIES OF THE WORLD

Five of the continents of the world are divided into countries. Most countries are now independent and manage their own affairs. A few of the smaller countries and islands are still ruled by another country.

Look at the boundaries between countries. Some follow natural features, such as rivers or mountain ranges. Straight boundaries were drawn for convenience. Often they separate people of the same language or tribe, and this can create problems.

The United Nations building, *in New York, USA. The world's problems are discussed – and sometimes solved – here. Almost every country has a representative at the United Nations.*

▼

Scale along the equator 1:116 000 000

0   1000km   2000km   3000km   4000km   5000km

1cm on the map = 1160 kilometres on the ground

0   1000miles   2000 miles   3000 miles

1inch on the map = 1860miles on the ground

Fact box

Only five of the 'top ten' countries with large populations are also among the 'top ten' biggest countries. Check which they are.

Asia has $6\frac{1}{2}$* of the ten most populated countries – but only $2\frac{1}{2}$* of the 'top ten' biggest countries.
*USSR is in both Asia and Europe.

Top ten countries by size	square kilometres
1 USSR	22,402,200
2 Canada	9,976,140
3 China	9,597,000
4 USA	9,363,123
5 Brazil	8,511,965
6 Australia	7,686,848
7 India	3,287,590
8 Argentina	2,776,889
9 Sudan	2,505,813
10 Algeria	2,381,741

Top ten countries by population (UN figures)	number of people
1 China	1085 million
2 India	790 million
3 USSR	283 million
4 USA	242 million
5 Indonesia	170 million
6 Brazil	140 million
7 Japan	121 million
8 Bangladesh	106 million
9 Pakistan	106 million
10 Nigeria	102 million

PEOPLE OF THE WORLD

Where People Live

- Very few or no people
- Few people
- More people
- Many people
- Very many people: the most crowded areas
- • Large cities: over 1 million people
- ■ Very large cities : over 5 million people

COPYRIGHT. GEORGE PHILIP & SON. LTD

There is *one* race of people: the human race. In Latin, we are all known as *Homo sapiens* – 'wise person'. The differences between people, such as dark or light skin, hair and eyes, are quite small.

But the differences in wealth are enormous. In any one country there are rich and poor people; but the differences between countries are even greater. The poorest countries are in the Tropics – especially in Africa (south of the Sahara) and south Asia. People are about fifty times richer in some countries of the Middle East and northwest Europe, Japan, the USA and Canada. These are the world's richest countries.

Watering onions in the Gambia, West Africa. *This boy's watering-can was given by the 'Freedom from Hunger Campaign', to help the family grow more food. Many schemes like this are helped by money from people in the rich countries of the world.*

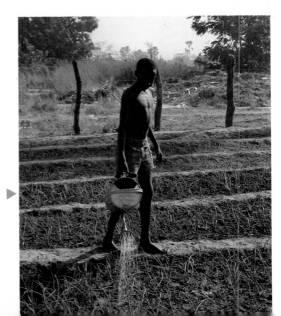

The main map (*opposite*) shows where the world's people live. Most of the world has very few people: notice that large areas are shown in yellow. Compare these areas with the maps on pages 6–7 and 14–15 and you will see that they are mostly desert, or high mountains, or densely forested, or very cold. So some remaining areas, where crops grow well, are very crowded indeed. Over half the world's people live in the lowlands of south and east Asia. Other crowded areas are parts of northwest Europe, the Nile valley and northeast USA. The most crowded places of all are the big cities.

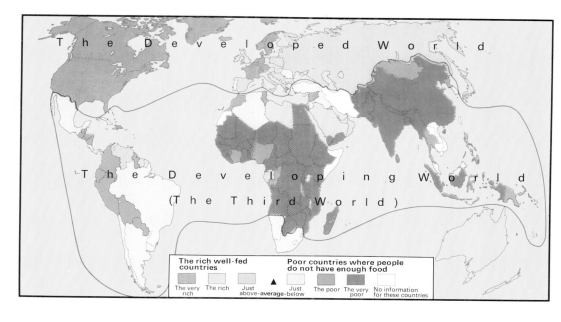

Empty and poor: nomads in the Sahara. *Bedouin nomads drink a cup of tea in the Sahara desert. They may be poor, but they are ready to welcome and help other travellers. The world's deserts are empty except where crops can be irrigated – as in the Nile valley.*

Crowded and rich: New York city. *The offices of Manhattan Island, in the centre of New York, are crowded with workers during the day, but are empty at night. Only the richest people can afford to live in apartments here.*

Crowded and poor: shanty town in Brazil. *These shanties on a steep hillside in Rio de Janeiro were built by people who have nowhere else to live. Poverty in the countryside forces people to the cities, but it is hard to find a job if you have no skills.*

The smaller map (*above*) shows those parts of the world where people get enough to eat, and where they are hungry. Some of the poorest people live in shanty towns (see below).

HOT AND COLD LANDS

Five important lines are drawn across these maps of the world: the Arctic and Antarctic Circles; the Tropics of Cancer and Capricorn; and the Equator. They divide the world roughly into the *polar*, *temperate* and *tropical* zones.

◀ **Arctic winter.** *Winter begins early in Greenland. These fishing boats are frozen in the harbour at Angmagssalik. From late September the days get shorter, until there are 24 hours of dark and cold at Christmas-time.*

The *polar* lands remain cold all through the year, even though the summer days are so long that the snow can melt.

The *tropical* lands are always hot, except where mountains or plateaus reach high above sea-level. For some of the year the Sun is directly overhead.

The *temperate* lands have four seasons: summer and winter, with spring and autumn in between. But these seasons come at different times of the year north and south of the Equator.

North of the Arctic Circle the sun does not set at all on June 21st.

Arctic Circle

NORTH AMERICA

EUROPE

ASIA

Al Aziziyah
The warmest place on earth

Tropic of Cancer

At the Tropic of Cancer the sun shines right overhead at noon on June 21st.

AFRICA

Equator

SOUTH AMERICA

Tropic of Capricorn

AUSTRALIA

Northern limit of snowfall

Hot and Cold in June

- Very hot
- Hot
- Warm
- Cool
- Cold
- Very cold
- Frozen seas

Vostok
The coldest place in the world.

South of the Antarctic Circle the sun does not even appear above the horizon on June 21st.

Antarctic Circle

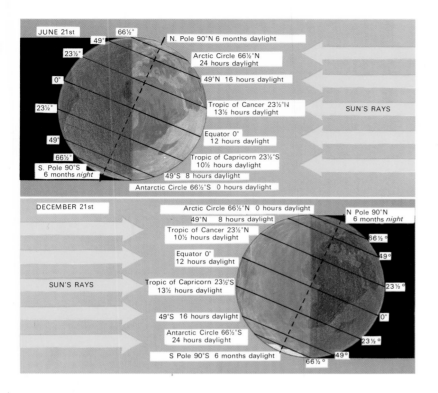

JUNE 21st
- N. Pole 90°N 6 months daylight
- Arctic Circle 66½°N 24 hours daylight
- 49°N 16 hours daylight
- Tropic of Cancer 23½°N 13½ hours daylight
- Equator 0° 12 hours daylight
- Tropic of Capricorn 23½°S 10½ hours daylight
- 49°S 8 hours daylight
- Antarctic Circle 66½°S 0 hours daylight
- S. Pole 90°S 6 months *night*

66½° 49° 23½° 0° 23½° 49° 66½°

SUN'S RAYS

DECEMBER 21st
- Arctic Circle 66½°N 0 hours daylight
- 49°N 8 hours daylight
- Tropic of Cancer 23½°N 10½ hours daylight
- Equator 0° 12 hours daylight
- Tropic of Capricorn 23½°S 13½ hours daylight
- 49°S 16 hours daylight
- Antarctic Circle 66½°S 24 hours daylight
- S Pole 90°S 6 months daylight
- N Pole 90°N 6 months *night*

66½° 49° 23½° 0° 23½° 49° 66½°

SUN'S RAYS

Fact box

Hottest recorded temperature 58°C at Al Aziziyah in Libya

Coldest recorded temperature −89.2°C at Vostok in Antarctica

Greatest change of temperature at one place in a year From −70°C to +36.7°C at Verkhoyansk in Siberia, USSR

Highest rainfall in 1 month and in 1 year 9299 mm in 1 month and 26,461 mm in 1 year at Cherrapunji, northwest India (see map page 14)

Most rainy days 350 days in a year at Mount Wai-'ale-'ale in Hawaii (see map page 14)

Wettest place on average Over 1 metre of rain a year at Tutunendo in Colombia (see map page 14)

Driest place In the Atacama desert, northern Chile, with *no* rain for 400 years! (See map page 14)

Most thunder 322 days in a year with thunder at Bogor in Java, Indonesia

The diagrams above help to explain why the seasons vary north and south of the Equator. In June (*top*) the Sun is overhead at the Tropic of Cancer. The North Pole is tilted towards the Sun, and the Arctic enjoys 24 hours of daylight. It is summer in North America, Europe and Asia. Notice that Antarctica is in total darkness.

By December, the Earth has travelled half-way round the Sun. Spot the difference in December (*below*). Where is the Sun overhead? Now Antarctica has 24 hours of daylight. It is summer in the southern continents, so children in Australia open Christmas presents in their summer holidays (see page 85).

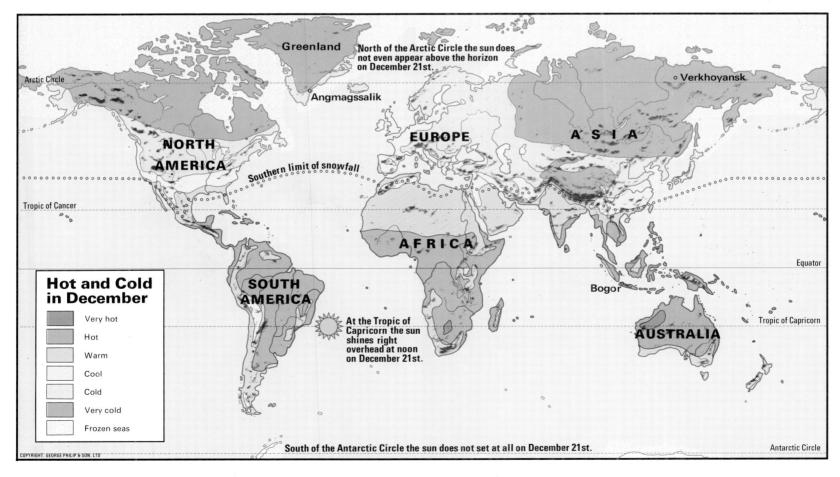

Greenland

North of the Arctic Circle the sun does not even appear above the horizon on December 21st.

Arctic Circle

Verkhoyansk

Angmagssalik

NORTH AMERICA

EUROPE

ASIA

Southern limit of snowfall

Tropic of Cancer

AFRICA

Equator

Hot and Cold in December

- Very hot
- Hot
- Warm
- Cool
- Cold
- Very cold
- Frozen seas

SOUTH AMERICA

Bogor

At the Tropic of Capricorn the sun shines right overhead at noon on December 21st.

Tropic of Capricorn

AUSTRALIA

South of the Antarctic Circle the sun does not set at all on December 21st.

Antarctic Circle

WET AND DRY LANDS

▲
Burning the savanna, *in northern Ghana, West Africa. At the end of the long dry season, farmers burn the bush (long grass and small trees). The land will be ready for planting crops as soon as the wet season begins.*

Water is needed by all living things. The map below shows that different parts of the world receive different amounts of water. Follow the Equator: most places near the Equator are very wet as well as being very hot. The map opposite shows that near the Equator there are large areas of thick forest. Here, it rains almost every day. Now follow the Tropic of Cancer and the Tropic of Capricorn on both maps. The Tropics cross areas of desert, where it is dry all year. Between the desert and the forest is an area of tall grass and bushes called the savanna. People here talk about the 'wet' and 'dry' seasons. For part of the year it is as rainy as at the Equator; for the rest of the year it is as dry as the desert.

North of the Sahara desert is the Mediterranean Sea. Places around this sea have lovely hot, dry summers, but they do have rain in winter. There are areas near other deserts with a similar climate, such as California in North America and central Chile in South America.

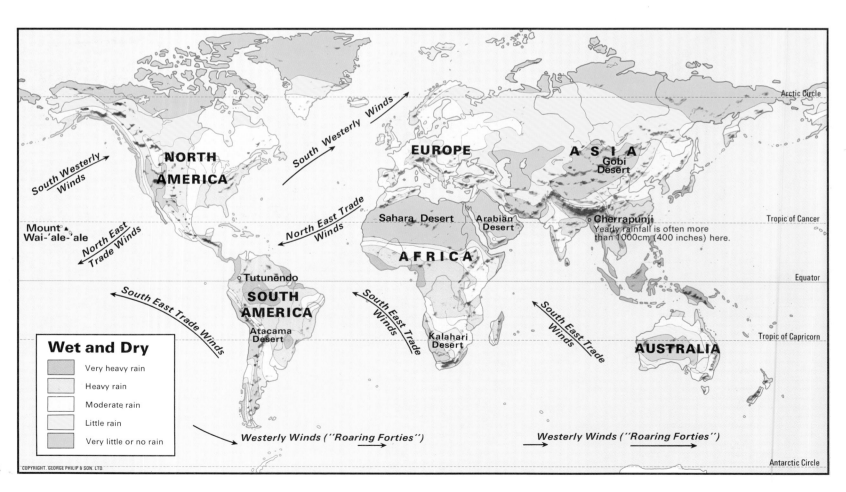

Wet and Dry

- Very heavy rain
- Heavy rain
- Moderate rain
- Little rain
- Very little or no rain

Forest and mountains in Alberta, Canada. The coniferous trees can survive Canada's bitterly cold winters. In the high mountains, trees cannot grow: it is too cold and the soil is too thin. Similar forests stretch across northern Europe and Asia, in Scandinavia and the USSR. The wood may be used for paper for books.

Desert in Namibia, southern Africa. The Namib Desert has given its name to the country of Namibia. It is a very dry area, west of the Kalahari desert. Winds usually blow away from the land, so rain is very rare.

In the temperate lands, many places have some rain all through the year. Damp winds from the sea bring plenty of rain to the coastal areas, and trees grow well. London and New York have some rain every month. Far inland, near the centre of the continents, and where high mountains cut off the sea winds, it is much drier. Here, there are vast grasslands, like the prairies of North America.

The Arctic and Antarctic lands are nearly as dry as the hot deserts. But the moisture collects as snow. Where the snow melts in the short summer, flowers and small plants grow in the marshy soil – called the tundra.

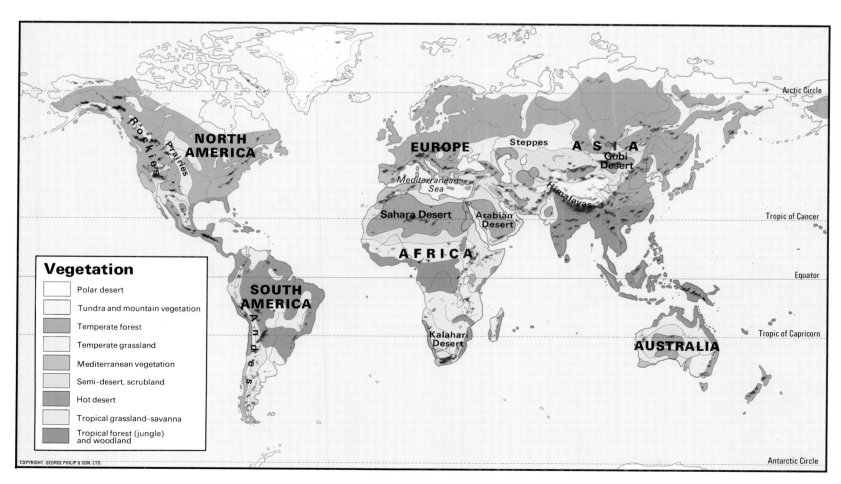

Vegetation

- Polar desert
- Tundra and mountain vegetation
- Temperate forest
- Temperate grassland
- Mediterranean vegetation
- Semi-desert, scrubland
- Hot desert
- Tropical grassland-savanna
- Tropical forest (jungle) and woodland

ENJOYING MAPS

An atlas is a book of maps. The maps in this book have been carefully drawn by cartographers (map-makers) to tell us about the countries of the world.

The maps on pages 6 to 15 show the whole world. Because the world is round, the best model is a globe. It is impossible to draw a really accurate map of the round world on a flat piece of paper. This is why the Pacific Ocean is cut in half, and Antarctica becomes a long thin strip. On pages 88 and 89 there are maps of parts of the world viewed from a different angle.

The maps on pages 18 to 89 show the continents and countries of the world. Each map has a key, with information that will help you 'read' the map. Use your imagination to 'see' what the land is like in each part of the world that you visit through these pages. The photos and text will make your picture clearer.

These two pages explain the key to all the maps. The country of Ghana is used as an example. Ghana is in square

The border between Ghana and Burkina Faso.
The red lines on the map show the boundaries between countries. When travelling from one country to another, you have to stop at the border. These children live in Ghana, and the Ghana flag is flying on their side of the border.

The message on the arch says 'Bye-bye; safe journey'. In Ghana, most officials speak English, and people drive on the left. But in Burkina Faso officials speak French and people drive on the right.

B2 of the map *(right)*. Find ⚑ at the top of the map with one finger, and ➋ at the side of the map with another finger. Move each finger in the direction of the arrows; Ghana is where they meet. The stamps and photograph on this page come from Ghana.

The capital city of each country is underlined in red on the maps. The rulers of the country live in the capital city, and it is the biggest city in most countries. But not all capital cities are big. On this map, you can see three sizes of city. The biggest ones are marked by a square; they have over one million people. Middle-sized cities have a big dot, and smaller cities have a small dot. Small towns and villages are not shown on maps of this scale, but some have been included in this atlas because they are mentioned in the text.

Countries that are coloured bright yellow on the map are shown in more detail on other pages. The small inset map shows where the main map fits into the continent of Africa. Maps of the whole of Africa are at the beginning of the Africa section (pages 52–3).

This is your chance to explore Africa – enjoy yourself!

Postage stamps

Postage stamps are on many pages of this atlas. You can learn so much from stamps! For example: the map shows you that Ghana is a country; the stamps tell you the official language of Ghana, and show you Ghana's flag.

The map tells you the name of Ghana's biggest lake (man-made). The 6Np stamp shows you the dam and tells you its name.

The map tells you that Ghana has a coastline; the 10Np stamp tells you the name of Ghana's main port, and shows you the big modern cranes there. Np stands for new pesewas (100 pesewas = 1 cedi).

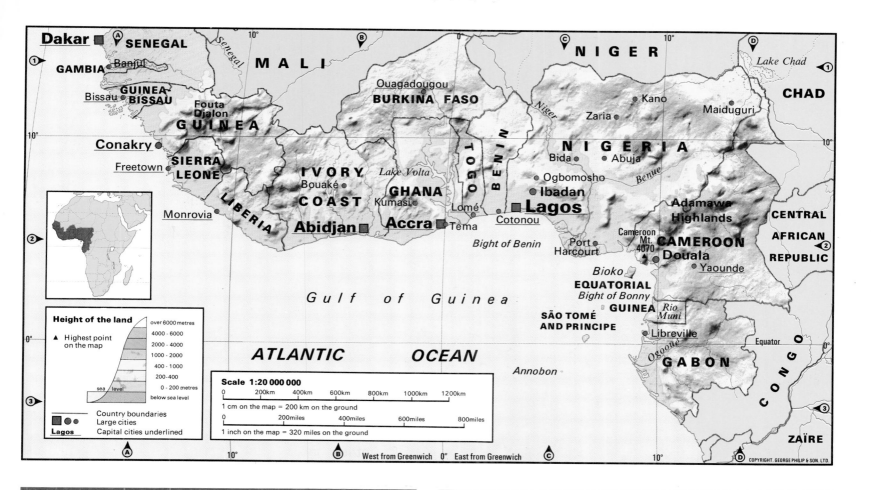

Map labels (West Africa):

Dakar ■ · SENEGAL · GAMBIA · Banjul · GUINEA-BISSAU · Bissau · Senegal · MALI · Ouagadougou · BURKINA FASO · NIGER · Lake Chad · CHAD · Kano · Zaria · Maiduguri · Niger · Fouta Djalon · GUINEA · Conakry · SIERRA LEONE · Freetown · Bouaké · IVORY COAST · Lake Volta · GHANA · Kumasi · TOGO · BENIN · Lomé · Cotonou · NIGERIA · Bida · Abuja · Ogbomosho · Ibadan · Lagos · Accra · Tema · Adamawa Highlands · CENTRAL AFRICAN REPUBLIC · Monrovia · LIBERIA · Abidjan · Bight of Benin · Port Harcourt · Cameroon Mt. 4070 ▲ · CAMEROON · Douala · Yaounde · Bioko · EQUATORIAL GUINEA · Bight of Bonny · SÃO TOMÉ AND PRINCIPE · Rio Muni · Libreville · Equator · Gulf of Guinea · ATLANTIC OCEAN · Annobon · Ogooué · GABON · CONGO · ZAÏRE

West from Greenwich 0° East from Greenwich

COPYRIGHT, GEORGE PHILIP & SON. LTD.

Height of the land (legend):
- over 6000 metres
- 4000 - 6000
- 2000 - 4000
- 1000 - 2000
- 400 - 1000
- 200 - 400
- 0 - 200 metres
- below sea level
- ▲ Highest point on the map
- sea level

Country boundaries
Large cities
Lagos Capital cities underlined

Scale 1:20 000 000

| 0 | 200km | 400km | 600km | 800km | 1000km | 1200km |

1 cm on the map = 200 km on the ground

| 0 | 200miles | 400miles | 600miles | 800miles |

1 inch on the map = 320 miles on the ground

Scale

Scale 1:20 000 000

| 0 | 200km | 400km | 600km | 800km | 1000km | 1200km |

1 cm on the map = 200 km on the ground

| 0 | 200miles | 400miles | 600miles | 800miles |

1 inch on the map = 320 miles on the ground

This box shows the scale of the map. The scale is written in different ways. The map is drawn to a scale of 1:20,000,000, which means that the distance between two places on the ground is exactly twenty million times bigger than it is on this page! Other maps in this atlas are drawn to different scales: little Belgium (page 24) is drawn at a scale of 1:2 million, while the largest country in the world is drawn at a scale of 1:45 million (USSR, page 38). Another way of writing the scale of this map is to say that 1 centimetre on the map is equal to 200 kilometres on the ground in West Africa. And this is how the scale line is drawn.

You can use the scale line to make your own scale ruler. Put the straight edge of a strip of paper against the scale line and mark the position of 200, 400, 600 kilometres, etc. (Or use the scale in miles if you prefer.) Carefully number each mark. Now move your scale ruler over the map to see how far it is between places. For example, Accra to Abidjan is 400 kilometres.

Height of the land

Height of the land (legend):
- over 6000 metres
- 4000 - 6000
- 2000 - 4000
- 1000 - 2000
- 400 - 1000
- 200 - 400
- 0 - 200 metres
- below sea level
- ▲ Highest point on the map
- sea level

Country boundaries
Large cities
Lagos Capital cities underlined

The countries of West Africa are coloured so that you can tell the height of the land. Green shows the lowest land.

Often the real land will not look green – in the dry season the grass is brown. The higher land is coloured yellow or brown, even though some parts are covered with thick green forest! The highest point in West Africa is shown with a small black triangle – find it in square C2 – but the mountains are not high enough to be shown in mauve or white: look for these on page 44. And to find land *below* sea-level, try page 24. Cameroon has some dramatic mountains (see page 57), but elsewhere the change from lowland to highland is often quite gentle.

Water features are shown in blue, and their names are in *italic print*. These include the sea, big rivers and lakes, such as Lake Chad (D1) and Lake Volta (B2). Blue dashes show rivers which dry up for some of the year.

EUROPE

The map shows the great North European plain that stretches from the Atlantic Ocean to the USSR. This plain has most of Europe's best farmland, and many of the biggest cities. To the north of the plain are the snowy mountains of Scandinavia. To the south are even higher mountains: the Pyrenees, the Alps and Carpathians, and the Caucasus Mountains of the USSR.

Southern Europe has hills and mountains by the Mediterranean Sea. The small areas of lowland are carefully farmed.

Puzzle picture

Western Europe's most important building.
★What building is it?
★Where is it?
★Why does it look so strange?
(Answers on page 96.)

These twelve car-plates are from the twelve countries of the European Community (Common Market). Can you name them?

(Answers on page 96.)

Height of the land

▲ Highest point on the map

over 6000 metres
4000 - 6000
2000 - 4000
1000 - 2000
400 - 1000
200-400
0 - 200 metres
sea level
below sea level

Deeper blue - deeper sea

Jan Mayen

ARCTIC OCEAN

North Cape

Lapland

Arctic Circle

Iceland

White Sea

Ural Mountains

ASIA

Faroe Is.

N. Dvina

Scandinavia

Shetland Is.

ATLANTIC

Orkney Is.

Hebrides

Gulf of Bothnia

Lake Ladoga

Gulf of Finland

British Isles

Baltic Sea

Ireland

Great Britain

North Sea

Central Russian Uplands

Volga Uplands

OCEAN

English Channel

Elbe

North European Plain

Vistula

Oder

Seine

Rhine

Loire

Carpathians

Dnepr

Ukraine

Volga

CASPIAN SEA

Bay of Biscay

Po

Danube

Crimea

Caucasus

Cape Finisterre

The Alps

Mt. Elbrus 5633

Iberian

Pyrenees

Dinaric Alps

BLACK SEA

Tagus

Corsica

Adriatic Sea

Bosporus

Peninsula

Balkans

Cape St. Vincent

Balearic Is.

Sardinia

Dardanelles

Anatolia

Strait of Gibraltar

Aegean Sea

ASIA

MEDITERRANEAN

Sicily

Malta

Crete

Cyprus

SEA

AFRICA

Scale 1:30 000 000

| 0 | 300km | 600km | 900km | 1200km | 1500km |

1 cm on the map = 300 km on the ground

| 0 | 300miles | 600miles | 900miles |

1 inch on the map = 480 miles on the ground

West 5 from Greenwich 0   5°

East from Greenwich 30°

COPYRIGHT. GEORGE PHILIP & SON. LTD.

18

West Germany/Austria border. *There are many contrasts in Europe. This photograph shows farmland (foreground); woodland (centre); and mountains (the Alps, in the background); find the Alps on the map on page 18. Another important contrast is not visible. The foreground is in West Germany, a big country; the background is in Austria, a small country.*

▼

Fact box: Europe

Area 10,531,000 square kilometres (including European USSR)

Highest point Mt Elbrus (USSR), 5633 metres

Lowest point Land reclaimed from the sea in the Netherlands is still below sea-level

Longest river Volga (USSR), 3690 kilometres

Largest lake Caspian Sea* (USSR), 360,700 square kilometres

Biggest country USSR*, 22,402,200 square kilometres (total area)

Smallest country Vatican City* (in Rome, Italy), less than half a square kilometre

Richest country Switzerland

Poorest country Albania

Most crowded country Malta

Least crowded country Iceland

*A *world record* as well as a European record

BRITISH ISLES

Scale 1:5 000 000

0   50km   100km   150km   200km   250km

1 cm on the map = 50 km on the ground

0   50miles   100miles   150miles

1 inch on the map = 80 miles on the ground

Height of the land

	over 6000 metres
	4000 - 6000
	2000 - 4000
	1000 - 2000
	400 - 1000
	200-400
sea level	0 - 200 metres
	below sea level

▲ Highest point on the map

Country boundaries
■ ● ● Large cities
London Capital cities underlined

Orkney Islands

Shetland Islands
60°

Wick

Hebrides

Lewis

North West Highlands

Skye

Inverness

Ben Nevis 1343
Grampians

Aberdeen

SCOTLAND

Mull
Oban
Dundee
Perth

Firth of Forth

Glasgow ■   ■ **Edinburgh**

Islay

ATLANTIC

Arran

OCEAN

Southern Uplands

Newcastle

Londonderry

NORTHERN
L. Neagh   ● Belfast
IRELAND
Armagh

Carlisle   ● Sunderland

Middlesbrough

Achill Sound

Isle of Man

Douglas

IRELAND   *Irish Sea*

York
Bradford   ● **Leeds**   ● Hull

● Galway   ● Athlone

Anglesey

Manchester

UNITED

Dublin

Holyhead

Liverpool   **Sheffield**

KINGDOM

North

Sea

Shannon

Snowdon 1085

Stoke-on-Trent   Derby   Nottingham

The Wash

Wicklow Mts.

Waterford   ● Wexford

E N G L A N D

Norwich

Cork

W A L E S

Birmingham ■

Coventry

Cambridge

Saint George's Channel

Aberystwyth

Worcester ●   *Avon*   Northampton ●

Ipswich

Wye

Gloucester

Luton

Cotswolds

● Oxford

Swansea

Thames   ■ **London**

Cardiff   **Bristol**

Reading

Port Talbot

Canterbury ●

Bristol Channel

Dover ●

Strait of Dover

BELGIUM

NETHERLANDS

Southampton
Brighton
Bournemouth
Portsmouth

Exeter ●

Isle of Wight

Plymouth ●

English Channel

FRANCE

Land's End   ● Penzance

Isles of Scilly

West from Greenwich 0° East from Greenwich

COPYRIGHT. GEORGE PHILIP & SON. LTD

The Highlands of Scotland *are beautiful. The hard rocks are hundreds of millions of years old, and they were eroded by glaciers in the Ice Age.*

Often, clouds cover the mountains, and there is a lot of rain. It is hard to make a living there.

20

What do the flags mean?

The Union Jack is made up of three flags: the red-on-white cross (+) of St George (England); the white-on-blue cross (×) of St Andrew (Scotland); and the red-on-white cross (×) of St Patrick (Ireland) – although most of Ireland is independent! St David (Wales) is not included, even though Wales is part of the UK.

The Republic of Ireland flag shows a white stripe (for peace) between orange (Protestants) and green (Roman Catholics).

Industry in South Wales. *This is the BP chemical works at Port Talbot, between Swansea and Cardiff. The big towers are cooling towers. The tall chimney on the right is part of the power station for the site. You can see sand-dunes in the foreground.*

The Cotswolds, England, *are limestone hills. A little village built long ago from the limestone rock nestles at the foot of the hill, where a spring gives pure water. Woodland, grassland and ploughed land still cover much of England.*

The United Kingdom is made up of Great Britain (England, Scotland and Wales) and Northern Ireland. The UK was the most important country in the world 150 years ago. Many old factories and coal-mines have now closed down, and several million people have no jobs. Unemployment is worst in the north. Much of the UK is still quiet and beautiful (see photograph above).

The Republic of Ireland is a completely separate country from the UK. There were twice as many people in Ireland 150 years ago as there are today. In the west, many abandoned farms can be seen. Farming is still important, and Irish butter and cream are famous. New factories have been built in many towns.

Ireland: harvesting reeds. *In the far west of Ireland, traditional scenes like this can sometimes still be seen. But tractors are more common nowadays. This view is near Achill Sound.*

Can you spot eight famous London landmarks on this stamp? (Answer on page 96.)

SCANDINAVIA

**Map labels:**

25°West from Greenwich 20° · 15°

ICELAND
Akureyri
65°
Vatnajokull
Reykjavik
Keflavik
Surtsey 20°
Vesteralen
Lofoten Islands

ARCTIC OCEAN

North Cape
Vardo
70°
Tromso
Kirkenes
L. Inari
Lapland
Narvik
Torne
Muonio
Bodo
Kiruna
Arctic Circle
Lule
Kemi
Lulea
Oulu
L. Oulu

N O R W A Y
S W E D E N
FINLAND

Trondheim
Ostersund
Storsjon
Alesund
Vaasa
Kuopio
Galdhopiggen 2469
Jotunheimen
Sundsvall
Sogne Fjord
Glama
Bergen
Lillehammer
Mjosa L.
Hardanger Fjord
Sørfjord
Oslo
Gavle
Aland Is.
Tampere
L. Sainiaa
Turku
Helsinki
Stavanger
Uppsala
Vasteras
Orebro
L. Vaner
Stockholm
Kristiansand
Norrkoping
U. S. S. R.
Skagen
Skagerrak
L. Vatter
Jonkoping
Gotland
Gothenburg
Aalborg
DENMARK
Jutland
Aarhus
Oland
Copenhagen
Esbjerg
Odense
Malmo
Sjælland
Bornholm
WEST GERMANY
EAST GERMANY
POLAND

Gulf of Bothnia
Baltic Sea
Gulf of Finland
Kattegat

Scale 1:10 000 000
0 100km 200km 300km 400km
1 cm on the map = 100 km on the ground
0 100miles 200miles
1 inch on the map = 160 miles on the ground

Height of the land
▲ Highest point on the map
over 6000 metres
4000 - 6000
2000 - 4000
1000 - 2000
400 - 1000
200 - 400
0 - 200 metres
sea level
below sea level
■ Country boundaries
●● Large cities
Oslo Capital cities underlined

COPYRIGHT. GEORGE PHILIP & SON. LTD

Land of ice and fire

Iceland has many volcanoes. Most are quiet and peaceful.
▼

EUROPA CEPT
ÍSLAND 85
JARDELDAR Á HEIMAEY 1973
ÍSLAND 25

But . . . sometimes a great volcanic eruption lights up the night sky and the light is reflected in the sea.

Only 240,000 people live in **Iceland**. It is near the Arctic Circle and there is ice on the mountains, in glaciers and ice-sheets. The sea stays ice-free and is full of fish. Iceland has an important fishing fleet.

▲
Sørfjord is a branch of Hardanger Fjord on the west coast of Norway. A fjord is a long, narrow, deep inlet of the sea with steep sides. Fjords were dug by valley glaciers in the Ice Age. Here the sides are so steep that the road is cut in solid rock. The cars show how steep and high the fjord sides are.

Forests and lakes in Finland.
Most of southern Finland is forested. The ice-sheets scraped hollows in the rocks and there are lots of beautiful lakes. The trees are cut down for timber, woodpulp, paper, chipboard, matches and other products that are sold abroad.

The mountains of Norway and Iceland are high and rugged. There are ice-sheets and glaciers even today. You can see snow on the highest land in the photograph of the fjord.

Southern Sweden and all of Denmark are lowland. This land was formed from sand and gravel brought by ice-sheets in the Ice Age. The sandy parts do not have good soil, but the clay lands grow very good crops.

The five countries of Scandinavia have small populations. Most people live in towns and cities, and hardly anyone is poor. There are very few people in Lapland in the far north, which lies inside the Arctic Circle.

Gothenburg *is the main port on* ▶ *the west coast of Sweden. The sea does not freeze here for long.*

Legoland *is a model village beside the Lego factory in Denmark. Everything is made of Lego! This is a model of a fishing village in the Lofoten Islands of Norway.*
▼

Reindeer in Lapland. *Lapland is the northern part of Norway, Sweden and Finland, where the Lapps live. They keep reindeer for their milk, meat and leather, and to pull sledges. Notice the warm and colourful clothes the Lapps wear.*

BENELUX

Bruges *is a historic town in Belgium. These old houses have survived many wars. Canals run through the town. The houses have no back door or garden — but they get a lovely view!*

COPYRIGHT. GEORGE PHILIP & SON LTD.

Spot the difference

What is the difference between these two coins from Belgium? And why is there a difference? (Answer on page 96.)

Europort, Rotterdam. *Rotterdam is by far the biggest port in the whole world: only a few of the docks can be seen here. Ships come from all over the world, and barges travel along the River Rhine and the canals of Europe to reach the port.*

Benelux is made up from *Bel*gium, *Ne*therlands and *Lux*embourg. Fortunately, the first two letters of each name are the same in most languages, so everyone can understand the word. These three countries agreed to co-operate soon after World War 2. But they still have their own King (of Belgium), Queen (of the Netherlands) and Grand Duke (of Luxembourg).

The Benelux countries are all small and are the most crowded in mainland Europe, but there is plenty of countryside too. Most of the land is low and flat, so they are sometimes called the Low Countries. But Luxembourg and eastern Belgium have pleasant wooded hills called the Ardennes. There are lots of modern industries, but the coalfield of central Belgium is a problem area because most of the coal-mines have closed.

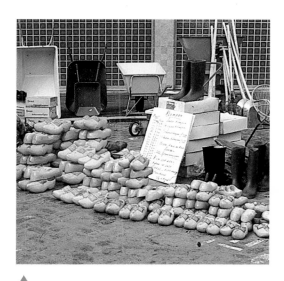

▲
Gouda market. *See the clogs for sale among the Wellingtons and wheelbarrows! Clogs are worn by some farmers and market gardeners, but many people prefer boots for working on the marshy land.*

Are these windmills?

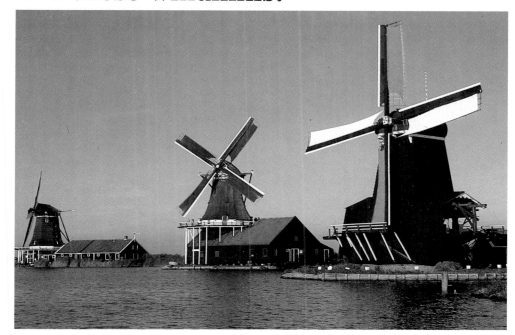

No, these are *not* windmills! They are really wind-*pumps*. They were used to pump water *up* from the fields into rivers and canals. The river is higher than the land! Much of the Netherlands was drained for farmland in this way. Nowadays, powerful diesel or electric pumps are used instead.

FRANCE

Height of the land

over 6000 metres	
4000 - 6000	
▲ Highest point on the map	2000 - 4000
	1000 - 2000
	400 - 1000
	200-400
sea level	0 - 200 metres
	below sea level

Country boundaries
■ ●● Large cities
PARIS Capital cities underlined

Scale 1:5 000 000

0   50km   100km   150km   200km   250km

1 cm on the map = 50 km on the ground

0   50miles   100miles   150miles

1 inch on the map = 80 miles on the ground

ATLANTIC OCEAN

Bay of Biscay

UNITED KINGDOM

■ London

English Channel

Alderney
Guernsey
Channel Islands (U.K.)
Jersey

Ushant
Brest

Cherbourg
Le Havre
Caen
St. Malo

Normandy

Brittany

Lorient
Rennes
Le Mans
Angers
St. Nazaire
■ Nantes

Tours
Loire

Poitiers

La Rochelle

Angoulême

Bordeaux
Garonne
Dordogne

Gascony

Bayonne
Lourdes

Toulouse

Pyrenees

SPAIN

ANDORRA

Dieppe
Amiens
Rouen

■ Paris
Seine
Chartres
Orléans
Bourges

Limoges

Clermont Ferrand

NETHERLANDS

Dunkirk
Calais
Boulogne
Lens
■ Lille
Douai
Valenciennes

Picardy

Reims
Troyes

Champagne

Dijon

Burgundy

Loire
Saône

BELGIUM

LUXEMBOURG

Thionville

Lorraine
Nancy
Metz

WEST GERMANY

Vosges
Strasbourg
Rhine
Moselle
Mulhouse
Montbéliard
Besançon

Jura

SWITZERLAND

Mt. Blanc 4807 ▲

■ Lyons
St. Étienne
Rhône

Massif Central

Auvergne

Cévennes

Languedoc

Nîmes
Montpellier

Carcassonne

Perpignan

Gulf of Lions

Grenoble

Valence

Orange
Avignon

Aix

Provence

ALPS

ITALY

MONACO
Nice
Cannes

Toulon

■ Marseilles

See page 32 for Corsica

MEDITERRANEAN SEA

Strait of Dover

6° A   4° B   4° C   2° D   0° E   2° F   4° G   6° H   8°

50°   48°   46°   44°   42°

2° East from Greenwich   0°   West from Greenwich 2°

French wine

A label from a bottle of French wine. The vines are growing in long straight rows on both sides of the valley. More wine is drunk in France than in any other country.

TOURAINE
SAUVIGNON

appellation TOURAINE contrôlée
VIN BLANC SEC ISSU DE CEPAGE SAUVIGNON
Mis en bouteille dans le Val de Loire
par C.V.L. à MONTREUIL BELLAY (France)
70cle
Produce of France

Market at Nice. *Which vegetables can you recognize on this stall? (Answer on page 96.) Every town in France has a good market. Housewives choose fresh fruit and vegetables very carefully.*

France is a country with three coastlines: can you see which these are? It is hot in summer in the south, but it is usually cool in the mountains and in the north. France is the biggest country in Western Europe, so there are big contrasts between north and south.

The highest mountains are the Alps in the southeast and the Pyrenees in the southwest. They are popular for ski-ing in winter and for summer holidays too. More than half the country is lowland, and farming is very important. Besides fruit, vegetables and wine, France is famous for its many different cheeses.

France is changing fast. The number of people living in villages is going down, and the population of the cities is growing — partly swelled by Arabs from North Africa who have come to live in France. The biggest city is Paris, which is also the capital. Ten million people now live in the Paris region, and five big new towns have been built around Paris.

Mont Blanc. *The 'White Mountain' is the highest mountain in Western Europe. It is 4807 metres high. Even in summer (as here) it is covered in snow. Cable-cars take tourists and skiers high up the mountain.*

Made in France

These *Majorette* models are made in France. They include a Renault van, a Michelin lorry, an Air France bus and a Paris bus. The most popular French cars are:

Renault   Citroen   Peugeot

What else can you find that is made in France? In our home we have:

BIC ball-point pens
a Le Creuset frying-pan
ARCOROC glassware
ARCOPOL cups and saucers
a MOULINEX mixer
and a Philips washing machine

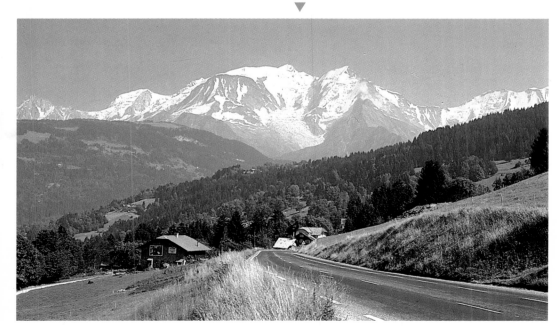

WEST AND EAST GERMANY AND AUSTRIA

The Rhine Gorge, *in West Germany. Castles once guarded this important river route. The Rhine flows north from Switzerland, through West Germany to the Netherlands. Big barges travel between the ports and factories by the river.*

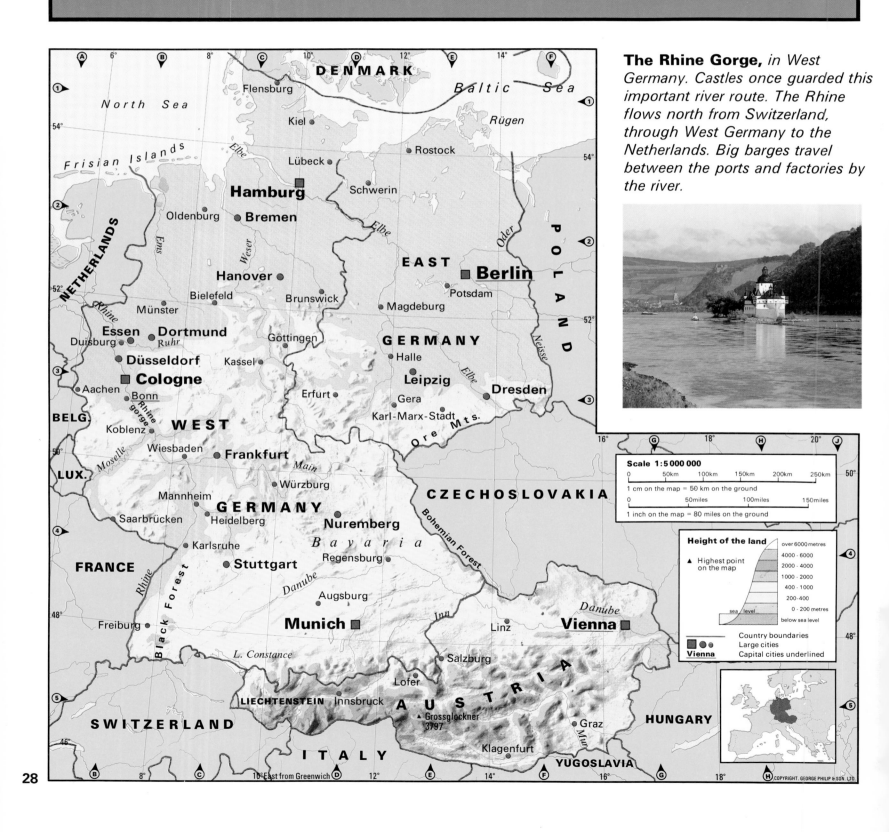

DENMARK

North Sea

Baltic Sea

Flensburg

Kiel

Rügen

Rostock

Frisian Islands

Lübeck

Schwerin

Elbe

Hamburg

Oldenburg • **Bremen**

Ems

Weser

Elbe

Oder

EAST

■ Berlin

Potsdam

P O L A N D

NETHERLANDS

Hanover

Bielefeld

Brunswick

Magdeburg

Göttingen

Neisse

G E R M A N Y

Essen • **Dortmund**

Münster

Duisburg

Ruhr

Halle

Düsseldorf

Kassel

Leipzig

Elbe

Cologne

Erfurt

Gera

Dresden

Aachen

Bonn

Rhine gorge

Karl-Marx-Stadt

Ore Mts.

BELG.

Koblenz

WEST

Moselle

Wiesbaden

Frankfurt

Main

LUX.

CZECHOSLOVAKIA

Würzburg

Mannheim

G E R M A N Y

Bohemian Forest

Saarbrücken

Heidelberg

Nuremberg

FRANCE

Karlsruhe

B a v a r i a

Stuttgart

Regensburg

Rhine

Black Forest

Danube

Augsburg

Danube

Freiburg

Inn

Linz

Vienna ■

L. Constance

Munich ■

Salzburg

LIECHTENSTEIN Innsbruck

A U S T R I A

Lofer

▲ Grossglockner 3797

Graz

SWITZERLAND

Mur

HUNGARY

I T A L Y

Klagenfurt

YUGOSLAVIA

East from Greenwich

Scale 1:5 000 000

0   50km   100km   150km   200km   250km

1 cm on the map = 50 km on the ground

0   50miles   100miles   150miles

1 inch on the map = 80 miles on the ground

Height of the land

over 6000 metres

4000 - 6000

2000 - 4000

▲ Highest point on the map

1000 - 2000

400 - 1000

200-400

0 - 200 metres

sea level

below sea level

Country boundaries

Large cities

Vienna   Capital cities underlined

West Germany has more people than any other European country. Most of the 60 million West Germans live in towns and cities. Several million people called 'guest workers' have come from southern Europe and Turkey to work in Germany's factories. But nowadays there is unemployment in West Germany, as in other European countries, and some 'guest workers' have returned home. Among the many different goods made in West Germany there are excellent cars: BMW, Opel, Porsche and Volkswagen.

There is also plenty of beautiful, uncrowded countryside. The north is mostly lowland; parts of the south are mountainous and popular for holidays, such as the Black Forest.

Sausages, beer and pretzels *are popular in West Germany. The beer from Munich is made from barley; the pretzels (dry biscuits) are made from wheat; the big sausages are made from pork.*

Transport stamps

East Germany has some double-decker trains so that more people can travel in comfort. West Germany has an amazing mono-rail: a single-rail railway which is built *above* the River Wupper. Both East and West Germany spend lots of money on good rail services.

The Alps *are popular for winter sports. This guesthouse in the village of Lofer, Austria, is full of skiers in winter. Trees cover the lower slopes of the mountains: the skiers will go up to the snow-slopes above the trees.*

Austria. Until 1918, Austria and Hungary were linked, and ruled a great Empire which included much of Central Europe. But now Austria is a small, peaceful country, which is friendly with both East and West Europe.

In the west of Austria are the high Alps, and many tourists come to enjoy the beautiful scenery and winter sports. Busy motorways and electric railways cross the Austrian Alps to link West Germany with Italy.

Most Austrians live in the lower eastern part of the country. The capital is Vienna. It was once near the centre of the Austrian Empire; now it is in a corner of the country.

East Germany. Until 1945, East and West Germany were one country, and Berlin was the capital city. To end World War 2 in 1945, Germany was invaded from west and east at the same time. The area invaded from the east by the USSR now forms East Germany. It still has close links with the USSR, and a communist government like the USSR. East Germany is smaller than West Germany and has fewer people: only 17 million.

Most of East Germany is lowland. Big deposits of coal, iron-ore and potash are mined. East Germany has fewer factories than West Germany, but more than other countries of East Europe.

Berlin is one city divided between two countries. East Berlin is the capital of East Germany. But West Berlin is part of West Germany, even though it is surrounded by East Germany. West Berlin is the biggest city in West Germany – nearly 2 million people live there. The Berlin Wall separates West Berlin from East Berlin.

The international clock *in East Berlin, which tells the time of the whole world! It is 16.00 hours (4 pm) in Berlin: what time is it in Reykjavik (Iceland)? And in Helsinki (Finland)? And how does the clock work?*
(Answers on page 96.)

29

SPAIN AND PORTUGAL

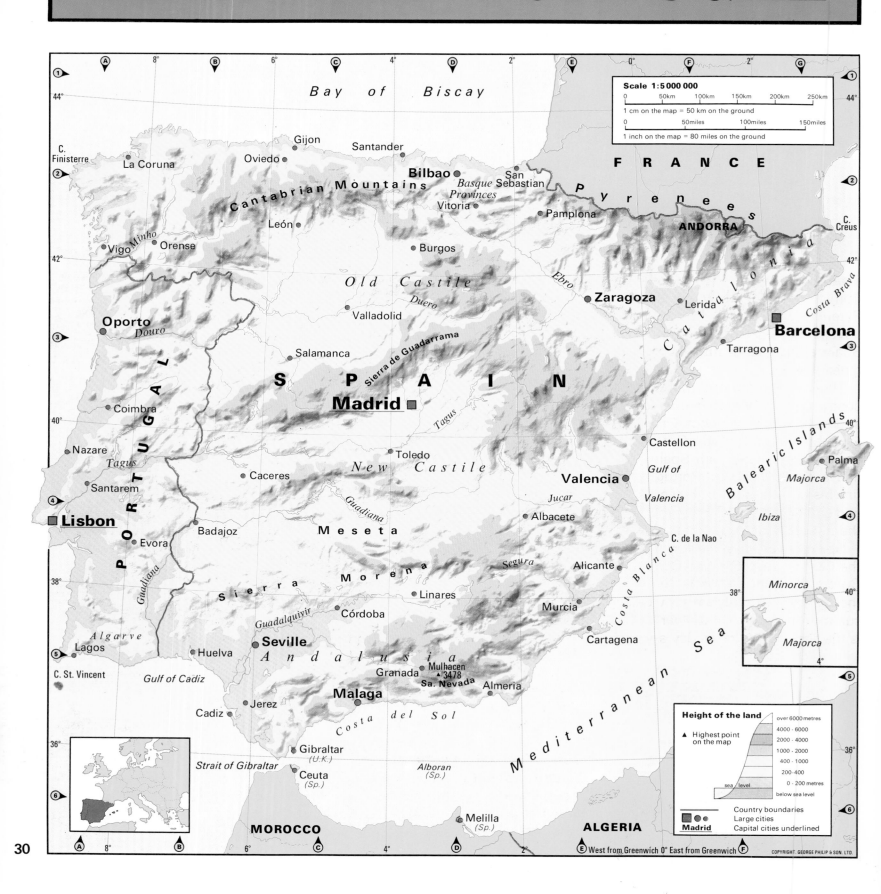

Bay of Biscay

Scale 1:5 000 000

| 0 | 50km | 100km | 150km | 200km | 250km |

1 cm on the map = 50 km on the ground

| 0 | 50miles | 100miles | 150miles |

1 inch on the map = 80 miles on the ground

C. Finisterre
La Coruna
Gijon
Santander
Oviedo
Bilbao
San Sebastian
FRANCE
Cantabrian Mountains
Basque Provinces
Vitoria
Pamplona
Pyrenees
ANDORRA
C. Creus
León
Burgos
Old Castile
Duero
Ebro
Zaragoza
Lerida
Catalonia
Costa Brava
Vigo
Minho
Orense
Valladolid
Oporto
Douro
Salamanca
Sierra de Guadarrama
Barcelona
Tarragona
S P A I N
Coimbra
Madrid
Tagus
Castellon
P O R T U G A L
Nazare
Tagus
Santarem
Toledo
New Castile
Caceres
Guadiana
Jucar
Valencia
Gulf of Valencia
Balearic Islands
Palma
Majorca
Ibiza
Lisbon
Badajoz
Meseta
Albacete
Evora
Guadiana
C. de la Nao
Sierra Morena
Segura
Linares
Murcia
Costa Blanca
Alicante
Algarve
Lagos
Guadalquivir
Córdoba
Seville
A n d a l u s i a
Huelva
Cartagena
C. St. Vincent
Gulf of Cadiz
Granada
Mulhacen ▲ 3478
Sa. Nevada
Almeria
Mediterranean Sea
Malaga
Jerez
Cadiz
Costa del Sol
Gibraltar (U.K.)
Strait of Gibraltar
Alboran (Sp.)
Ceuta (Sp.)
MOROCCO
Melilla (Sp.)
ALGERIA

Minorca
Majorca

Height of the land

	over 6000 metres
	4000 · 6000
	2000 · 4000
▲ Highest point on the map	1000 · 2000
	400 · 1000
	200 · 400
	0 · 200 metres
sea level	below sea level

Country boundaries
Large cities
Madrid Capital cities underlined

30

West from Greenwich 0° East from Greenwich

COPYRIGHT GEORGE PHILIP & SON, LTD.

◄ Village in southern Spain. *The old houses crowd closely together, and roads are very narrow: wide enough for a donkey, but not for lorries. People whitewash their houses to reflect the rays of the hot sun. Olive trees grow on the hills.*

Did you know?

Gibraltar is still a British colony, but it is only 6 square kilometres in area. Spain still owns two towns in Morocco: *Ceuta* and *Melilla*. Spain wants Gibraltar – and Morocco wants Ceuta and Melilla. The arguments continue. . . .

Spain and Portugal are separated from the rest of Europe by the high Pyrenees mountains. Most people travelling by land from the north reach Spain along the Atlantic or Mediterranean coasts.

The Meseta is the high plateau of central Spain. Winters are very cold, and summers are very hot. Olives and vines are the main crops. But cars are the biggest export from Spain nowadays. Both Spain and Portugal have fine historic cities, with great churches and cathedrals – built when they were the richest countries in the world.

Spain is very popular for holidays: the Costa Brava (Rugged Coast), the Costa del Sol (Coast of the Sun), and the Balearic Islands are crowded in summer. In Portugal the Algarve coast is the most popular holiday area.

The Alhambra Palace, Granada. *This beautiful palace was built by the Moors (Arabs from North Africa). The Moors ruled southern Spain for hundreds of years, until 1492. The Arabs brought new crops and new ideas to Europe.*

▼

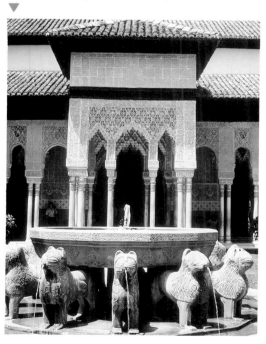

Spanish coins

Spain became a monarchy again in 1975; the coin shows King Juan Carlos I.

In 1982, the World Cup was held in Spain: this special coin shows a football and the world.

Bull-ring and flats, Malaga. *The bull-ring is a big and important building in Spanish cities. High blocks of flats are typical of modern Spain. In the background is the blue Mediterranean Sea. Malaga is a large port in southern Spain.*

▼

◄ Sun-dried fish, Portugal. *Sardines caught in the Atlantic Ocean are dried in the strong sunshine at Nazare, Portugal. Many of the older ladies wear black clothes, even in summer.*

SWITZERLAND AND ITALY

Labels from food exported from Italy: try making a collection yourself!

Sorano, *central Italy. Long ago the hill town was a safe place to live. The houses huddled closely round the castle and the church. Nowadays, a hill town needs a zigzag road to reach it.* ▶

Italy is shaped like a boot: its toe seems to be kicking Sicily! The shape is caused by the long range of fold-mountains called the Apennines. The great Roman Empire was centred on Italy, and there are many Roman ruins. Yet Italy was only united as a country less than 150 years ago. Italy has lots of big factories. The Fiat car plant in Turin is one of the largest and most modern in the world.

▲
Venice, *northeast Italy. Travel is by boat, or on foot: there are no cars, because the 'roads' are canals.*

Swiss record breakers

Switzerland holds some amazing world records.

*The *longest* road tunnel is the St Gotthard tunnel (16.32 kilometres).
*The *longest* stairway is beside the Niesenbahn mountain railway, near Spiez. It has 11,674 steps!
*The *highest* dam is the Grande Dixence Dam: 285 metres high.

*And Switzerland has been at peace with everyone since 1815. That's quite a record!

Switzerland also has the *oddest* car-plates: CH is from the Latin name for Switzerland:

CH

Confederatio *Helvetica.*

In **Switzerland** most people live in cities north of the Alps. Switzerland is one of the world's richest countries, with modern banks, offices and factories.

Rivers, dams and waterfalls in the Alps are used for making hydro-electric power: trains, factories and homes in Switzerland all run on cheap electricity. Cable-cars powered by electricity take skiers and tourists high into the beautiful mountains.

Lauterbrunnen valley, Switzerland. *This Alpine valley has been dug by a glacier. Notice the big waterfall.*

A

8°

Basle

Winterthur

FRANCE

Zurich

St. Gallen

LIECHTENSTEIN

WEST GERMANY

AUSTRIA

1

Luzern

Bern

Spiez

Interlaken

Rhine

SWITZERLAND

Tyrol

Inn

Lausanne

L. Geneva

St. Gotthard tunnel

Geneva

Rhône

Bolzano

Grande Dixence dam

46°

Lugano

Mte. 4634 Rosa

The Alps

Udine

46°

YUGOSLAVIA

L. Garda

Milan

Trieste

Brescia

Verona

F R A N C E

Turin

Po

Padua

Venice

2

Po

2

Parma

Genoa

Bologna

Ravenna

La Spezia

Rimini

Gulf of Genoa

SAN MARINO

Pisa

Florence

MONACO

Riviera

A P E N N I N E S

Ancona

Ligurian Sea

Siena

Perugia

YUGOSLAVIA

Adriatic

3

Bastia

3

Elba

Sorano

Corsica (France)

Terni

Tiber

Pescara

Sea

42°

Ajaccio

42°

Vatican City

Rome

ALBANIA

4

Foggia

4

Sassari

Bari

Naples

Vesuvius

Brindisi

Sardinia (Italy)

Salerno

Taranto

Strait of Otranto

40°

Gulf of Taranto

40°

Cagliari

Tyrrhenian Sea

Cosenza

Ionian Sea

5

5

M e d i t e r r a n e a n

Lipari Is.

38°

Palermo

Messina

38°

Egadi Is.

Reggio

S i c i l y

Mt. Etna

Str. of Messina

Catania

Siracusa

S e a

Pantelleria

6

TUNISIA

6

8°

B

10° East from Greenwich

C

12°

D

14°

E

16°

F

18°

COPYRIGHT. GEORGE PHILIP & SON. LTD

33

Gozo

MALTA Valletta

SOUTHEAST EUROPE

Most of southeast Europe is very mountainous, except near the River Danube. Farmers keep sheep and goats in the mountains and grow grain, vines and sunflowers on the lower land.

The coastlines are popular with tourists. There are many holiday resorts beside the Adriatic Sea (Yugoslavia), the Aegean Sea (Greece and Turkey) and the Black Sea (Romania and Bulgaria). All these countries are trying to develop industry, but this is still one of the poorest parts of Europe.

Albania is the least-known country in all Europe: very few people are allowed to visit it. No railways crossed the frontier of Albania until 1985.

Yugoslavia is 1 country with 2 alphabets (Latin and Cyrillic), 3 religious groups (Roman Catholic, Orthodox and Moslem), 4 languages, 6 republics and 7 neighbours (can you name them from the map?). It is the biggest country in southeast Europe.

▲
Dubrovnik *is an old town on the coast of Yugoslavia. The walls are very big and impressive.*

▲
Romania. *Behind the maize (sweetcorn) a huge modern factory brings jobs and money – and pollution too. The tractor and plough on the Romanian coin show that farming is still important. The Romanian language is not hard to understand. Try to read the words on the stamp.*

The Danube

The stamp shows a tourist boat at the gorge on the River Danube called the Iron Gates, on the border of Romania and Yugoslavia. The Danube flows eastwards for 1700 kilometres from West Germany to the Black Sea. It passes seven countries, and is becoming important for trade. Dams and locks now allow big ships to navigate the river.

◄ **Fishing village, Crete.** *Crete is the biggest of the many islands that form part of* **Greece***. The village nestles below the mountains. Some of the fishermen's cottages have become guesthouses for tourists.*

The Greek alphabet. *The Greeks developed their alphabet before the Romans, and they still use it. Some letters are the same as ours (A, B . . .), and some look the same but have a different sound (P, H . . .). The other letters are completely different. Some Greek letters appear in the Cyrillic alphabet, which is used in Bulgaria, Yugoslavia and the USSR (see page 39). The word* alphabet *is formed from the first two Greek letters:* alpha *and* beta.

Α Β Γ Δ Ε Ζ Η Θ Ι Κ Λ Μ Ν Ξ Ο Π Ρ Σ Τ Υ Φ Χ Ψ Ω

EAST EUROPE

DENMARK

Baltic Sea

Gdansk Bay

Gdansk ●

● Elblag

● Olsztyn

● Szczecin

● Bialystok

Oder

Vistula

Bydgoszcz ●

● Torun

Warta

Bug

EAST

WEST GERMANY

● Poznan

■ **Warsaw**

P O L A N D

Neisse

● **Lodz**

GERMANY

Radom ●

● Lublin

Wroclaw ●

Oder

Warta

● Czestochowa

● Kielce

Ore Mts.

Liberec ●

Ohre

Silesia

Vistula

● Bytom

Gliwice ● ● Katowice

Prague ■

Labe

Krakow ●

Carpathian

Plzen ●

Bohemia

C Z E C H O S L O V A K I A

● Bielsko-Biala

Ostrava ●

● Olomouc

▲Tatra 2655

Mountains

Bohemian Forest

Telc ●

Brno ●

Morava

● Kosice

Bratislava ●

Miskolc ●

Tisza

● Debrecen

AUSTRIA

● Gyor

■ **Budapest**

H U N G A R Y

Danube

U. S. S. R.

L. Balaton

ROMANIA

Drava

● Pecs

Szeged ●

Tisza

YUGOSLAVIA

Height of the land

▲ Highest point on the map

over 6000 metres	
4000 - 6000	
2000 - 4000	
1000 - 2000	
400 - 1000	
200 - 400	
sea level	0 - 200 metres
	below sea level

■ ● ● Country boundaries / Large cities

Warsaw Capital cities underlined

Scale 1:5 000 000

0 50km 100km 150km 200km 250km

1 cm on the map = 50 km on the ground

0 50miles 100miles 150miles

1 inch on the map = 80 miles on the ground

10° 12° East from Greenwich 14° 16° 18° 20° 22° COPYRIGHT. GEORGE PHILIP & SON. LTD.

What can you buy from Poland?

In our home, we have: shoes from Poland; chairs from Poland; books from Poland; and jam from Poland. What can *you* find from Poland?

◀ **Ploughing the fields, Poland.**
Horses are still used for ploughing fields in many parts of Poland. Look carefully . . . . How many horses are pulling the plough?

Czechoslovakia, Poland and Hungary are allied with the USSR in the Warsaw Pact (see stamp below). They have communist governments.

Poland has a coastline on the Baltic Sea. There are big shipbuilding factories at Gdansk, but most of Poland is flat farmland (see photograph above).

Czechoslovakia has beautiful hills and mountains. The lower slopes are covered with pine trees. The Czechs live in the west of the country, and the Slovaks in the east.

Hungary is a small, flat country. Mostly it is farmland, but Hungary also has the biggest bus-factory in the world. Buda and Pest were twin cities, on either side of the River Danube. Now they have become Budapest, the capital city (see photograph below). Polish, Czech and Slovak are Slavic languages. Hungarian is a totally different language; it came from central Asia. You can see some Hungarian words on the stamp.

Budapest, Hungary, *on the River Danube. A vintage paddle-steamer takes holidaymakers past the parliament building of Budapest, the capital city of Hungary.*
▼

Warsaw Pact countries

This Hungarian stamp shows the flags of the Warsaw Pact countries. The letters will help you guess the countries.

B	C*	R
H	M*	USSR
(E)G	P	C

Can you name them? Answers on page 96. (*Not in Europe.)

▲
Town square in Telc, Czechoslovakia. *The historic centres of towns are carefully preserved in Eastern Europe. Some have been totally rebuilt in the old style, after wartime bombing.*

USSR

Scale 1 : 45 000 000

| 0 | 450km | 900km | 1350km | 1800km |

1 cm on the map = 450 km on the ground

| 0 | 450miles | 900miles |

1 inch on the map = 720 miles on the ground

Height of the land

	over 6000 metres
▲ Highest point on the map	4000 - 6000
	2000 - 4000
	1000 - 2000
	400 - 1000
	200 - 400
sea level	0 - 200 metres
	below sea level

Country boundaries
●● Large cities
Moscow Capital city underlined

The USSR flag – the Red Flag

The hammer represents workers in industry, and the sickle represents farmworkers. The red colour represents the Communist Revolution.

USSR means
*U*nion of
*S*oviet
*S*ocialist
*R*epublics

The USSR is by far the biggest country in the world: it is bigger than Canada and the USA together! In fact it is the biggest country in Europe *and* the biggest country in Asia as well. It is made up of 15 separate republics: the largest is Russia.

The Siberian steppes. *A lonely horse-cart travels along a track in Siberia. The steppes are* not *steps! They are part of the world's biggest plain – snow-covered in winter, and with grass or wheat in summer.*

38

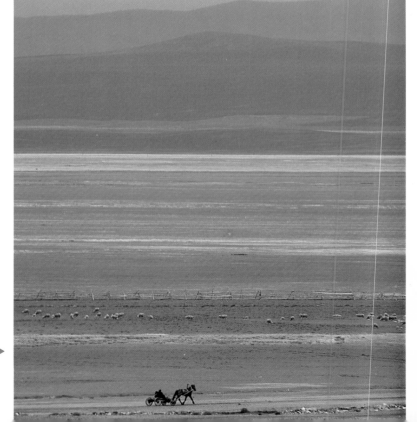

The USSR stretches across two continents, Europe and Asia. Most people live in the European part, west of the Ural Mountains. But gradually people are moving east to new towns.

Because the USSR is so huge, there are many different climates and almost all crops can be grown. The far north is snow-covered for most of the year (see page 89). Further south is the largest forest in the world – a vast area of coniferous trees stretching from the Baltic Sea to the Sea of Okhotsk. Grassy plains, called the steppes, come south of the forest. In some parts, grain is grown on huge farms. The south is desert, hot in summer but cold in winter. With irrigation, crops like sugar-cane and cotton grow well. And in the warm hills near the Caucasus Mountains, tea is an important crop. The USSR also has huge deposits of many different minerals and can supply most of the needs of its many different factories.

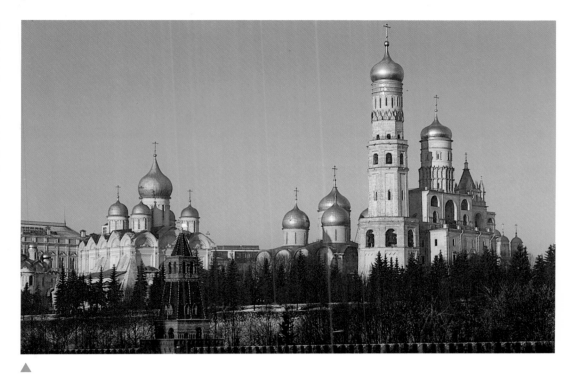

▲
The Kremlin, Moscow. *There are three former churches in the Kremlin; it now houses the government of the USSR. The golden domes can be seen far away.*

The Cyrillic alphabet

Russian is written in the Cyrillic alphabet. This is partly based on Latin letters (the same as English letters) and partly on Greek letters (see page 35).

The alphabet was invented centuries ago by St Cyril, so that the Russian church could show it was separated from both the Roman and the Greek churches. In Cyrillic, R is written P, and S is written C. So the Metro is written МЕТРО. СССР (on stamps and coins) is Russian for SSSR (Soyuz Sovetskikh Sotsialisticheskikh Respublik), the initials of the country in Russian.

▲
GUM shopping centre, Moscow. *Local people go to GUM for shopping. The buildings are fine – but there are still queues and shortages in USSR shops. GUM is short for Government Department Store in Russian.*

Trans-Siberian railway

It takes over a week to cross the USSR by train and you must change your watch seven times. Here is the distance chart and timetable (only the main stops are shown).

Distance in km	Town	Time (at Moscow)	Day
0	Moscow	14.30	1
957	Kirov	06.16	2
1818	Sverdlovsk	19.40	2
2716	Omsk	09.48	3
3343	Novosibirsk	19.55	3
4104	Krasnoyarsk	08.49	4
5184	Irkutsk	04.45	5
5647	Ulan Ude	13.07	5
6204	Chita	23.17	5
7313	Skovorodino	22.27	6
8531	Khabarovsk	22.35	7
9297	Vladivostok	13.15*	8

*This is 20.05 local time at Vladivostok.

Don't forget to allow another 8 days if you want to come back!

АБВГДЕЁЖЗИЙКЛМНОПРСТУФХЦЧШЩЪЭЮЯ

ASIA

Asia is the world's biggest continent, stretching from the cold Arctic Ocean in the north, to the warm Indian Ocean in the tropical south. Mainland Asia nearly reaches the Equator in Malaysia. Several Asian islands are *on* the Equator: Sumatra, Borneo and Sulawesi. In the west, Asia reaches Europe and the Mediterranean Sea, and in the east Asia reaches the Pacific Ocean, and gets close to Australia. In the centre are the high, empty plateaus of Tibet and Mongolia.

◄ **Himalayan Mountains, Nepal,** *photographed by the famous mountaineer Chris Bonington. The world's ten highest mountains are all in the Himalayas. Glaciers have carved the deep valleys.*

Height of the land

- over 6000 metres
- 4000 - 6000
- 2000 - 4000
- 1000 - 2000
- 400 - 1000
- 200 - 400
- 0 - 200 metres
- below sea level

Deeper blue - deeper sea

▲ Highest point on the map

Scale 1: 60 000 000

| 0 | 600km | 1200km | 1800km | 2400km | 3000km |

1 cm on the map = 600km on the ground

| 0 | 600miles | 1200miles | 1800miles |

1 inch on the map = 960 miles on the ground

East 100° from Greenwich 110°

COPYRIGHT. GEORGE PHILIP & SON. LTD.

Money in Asian

Afghanistan
Bangladesh
Bhutan
Burma
Cambodia
China
Cyprus
Indonesia
Iran
Israel
Japan
Korea, N and S
Laos
Lebanon, Syria
Macao
Maldives
Mongolia
Oman
Philippines
Qatar
Saudi Arabia
Sri Lanka
Thailand
Turkey
UAE
Vietnam

Fact box: Asia

Area 44,387,000 square kilometres (including Asiatic USSR)

Highest point Mount Everest* (Nepal/China), 8848 metres

Lowest point Shores of Dead Sea* (Israel/Jordan), 400 metres below sea-level

Longest river Yenisey (USSR), 5540 kilometres; Yangtze (China), 5530 kilometres

Biggest country USSR* 22,402,200 square kilometres

Smallest country The Maldives, 298 square kilometres

*A *world record* as well as an Asian record

Buddhist shrine. *Religion is very important to most people in Asia. This Buddhist shrine is like many found in Nepal. It has been decorated with prayer flags and painted eyes.* ▶

Two countries cover over half of Asia: the USSR and China. India looks quite small – yet it is over ten times as big as Italy or the UK! But some of Asia's important countries are very small indeed, for example Lebanon and Israel in southwest Asia (Middle East); Singapore and Brunei in southeast Asia (Far East).

Over half the world's population lives in Asia. The coastal areas of south and east Asia are the most crowded parts. Seven of the 'top ten' most populated countries in the world are in Asia: China, India, USSR, Indonesia, Japan, Bangladesh and Pakistan.

Some countries

Afghani
Taka
Ngultrum
Kyat
Riel
Yuan
Pound
Rupiah
Rial
Shekel
Yen

Won
Kip

Pound
Pataca
Rufiyaa
Tugrik
Rial
Peso
Riyal
Rial
Rupee
Baht
Lira
Dirham
Dong

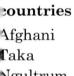

Scale 1 : 60 000 000

| 0 | 600km | 1200km | 1800km | 2400km | 3000km |

1 cm on the map = 600km on the ground

| 0 | 600miles | 1200miles | 1800miles |

1 inch on the map = 960 miles on the ground

U.A.E = United Arab Emirates

Asia in the World

East 100° from Greenwich 110°

COPYRIGHT GEORGE PHILIP & SON. LTD.

MIDDLE EAST

Scale 1:25 000 000

| 0 | 250km | 500km | 750km | 1000km | 1250km |

1 cm on the map = 250 km on the ground

| 0 | 250miles | 500miles | 750miles |

1 inch on the map = 400 miles on the ground

Height of the land

	over 6000 metres
▲ Highest point on the map	4000 - 6000
	2000 - 4000
	1000 - 2000
	400 - 1000
	200 - 400
sea level	0 - 200 metres
	below sea level

Country boundaries
Large cities
Tehran Capital cities underlined

COPYRIGHT. GEORGE PHILIP & SON. LTD.

◀ **Holy cities of the Middle East.**
In Jerusalem (*left*), Jews worship at the Wailing Wall, all that remains of the Jewish temple. *Jerusalem* is a holy city for people of three religions: Judaism, Christianity and Islam. People of all three religions live here and pilgrims and tourists visit the city.

Mecca (*right*) is the holiest city of ▶ Islam: it is where the prophet Mohammed was born. Moslems come from many countries to worship here.

Lands of the books

Three great religions started in the Middle East: Judaism, Christianity and Islam.

The Jewish scriptures are written in Hebrew. This is the world's oldest written language still in use today and reads from right to left across the page.

The Christian Bible consists of the Jewish scriptures (the Old Testament), plus the New Testament, which was originally written in Greek.

The Koran is the holy book of Islam. It is written in Arabic, which is also read from right to left.

The Jewish scriptures are written in Hebrew. ▼

The Koran is written in Arabic. ▼

▲
Oil in the Middle East. *The photograph above, taken in Iran, shows camels in the desert . . . a view that has not changed for centuries. But the flares and smoke in the distance are a clue to the biggest change in the Middle East: oil. Oil is pumped out from deep underground, and piped to ports for export to many countries in Europe, Asia and Africa. It is used for diesel, petroleum, paraffin and chemicals.*

The 'Middle East' is another name for 'southwest Asia'. It is the part of Asia which is closest to Europe and Africa. In fact, Turkey is partly in Europe. Of all the countries on this map, Turkey has the most people.

Most of the Middle East is semi-desert or desert. Yet many great civilizations have existed here, such as the Assyrian, the Babylonian and the Persian. Their monuments are found in the fertile valleys of the largest rivers, the Tigris and the Euphrates.

Scarce water is used to irrigate crops in some places. In others, herds of sheep and goats are kept. Dates from Iraq come from desert oases; oranges come from irrigated land in Israel.

▲
Progress in Qatar. *The big bulldozer was imported from England, to help build the new road. In the background you can see new skyscrapers and a big crane. Oil has made some countries in the Middle East very rich, especially those near The Gulf, like Saudi Arabia, Kuwait and Qatar.*

◀ **Winnowing wheat in Turkey.** *The gentle evening breeze separates the grain from the chaff: the heavier grain falls down, while the lighter chaff blows away. Winnowing is hard work! It has been done by hand for thousands of years: the old methods are still commonly used in many parts of the Middle East.*

SOUTH ASIA

The world's highest mountains appear on this map, including Mount Everest. The Himalayas form a great mountain chain which joins on to other high mountain areas, such as the Hindu Kush.

Afghanistan is a rugged and mountainous country. Five other countries share the peninsula which stretches southwards from the Himalayas. **Bhutan** and **Nepal** are small mountain kingdoms.

Bangladesh is quite different: it is mostly flat, low-lying land where the great rivers Ganges and Brahmaputra reach the sea. In the west, **Pakistan** is a desert country, but the River Indus is used to irrigate crops.

India is the largest country. It stretches 3300 kilometres from Kashmir to Cape Comorin. Until 1947, Pakistan and Bangladesh were part of the Indian Empire, ruled by Britain.

Sri Lanka is an island country off the south coast of India. Further south, in the Indian Ocean, a chain of islands makes up the country called **The Maldives.**

More than 1000 million people live in south Asia. The deserts and mountains do not have many people, but the river valleys, plains and plateaus are crowded.

Sri Lanka *means Resplendent Isle. This country used to be called* Ceylon. *Tea is an important crop in the hills where there is plenty of rain. Women pick the young leaves from the bushes* (right), *then they are dried and crushed and packed into tea-chests. Ceylon tea* (left) *is one of Sri Lanka's most important exports. Where does the tea you drink come from?*

44

Planting rice, Bangladesh. *These men are planting out rice seedlings in the wet soil. Sometimes monsoon floods can wash away the seedlings.*

Rice is an important food crop in south Asia. It grows best where the land is flat, and where the weather is hot and wet. The seeds are planted in a 'nursery' bed just before the monsoon rains are due (see below). When the fields are flooded, the seedlings are planted in the mud. In a good year, rice grows in the wet fields and is ready for harvesting after four or five months. If the monsoon fails and there is a drought, the seedlings will shrivel up. If the rice crop fails, many people go hungry. In areas where irrigation is available, the farmer can control the water supply and may be able to grow two rice crops a year.

Religion is very important in the lives of people in south Asia. Hinduism is the oldest religion, and most people in India and Nepal are Hindus. Buddhism began in India, but only Sri Lanka and Bhutan are mainly Buddhist today. Afghanistan, Pakistan and Bangladesh are Islamic countries. Many Sikhs live in northern India; there are also Christian groups in all these countries.

India's flag *shows that people of different religions are united in one country. The orange stripe is for Hindus; the green for Moslems; and the white for peace, with the wheel of Ashoka for Buddhists.*

Wool for carpets. *This lady in northern India is winding wool which will be used to make carpets. She sits in the courtyard of her house, where the ploughs and pots and pans are also kept.*

The monsoon

Most rain falls in one season, called the monsoon. In Bombay the monsoon begins in June (*left*) and the rain pours down for a few weeks (*right*). There are heavy showers in August and September, and then hardly any more rain until next June. From October to March the weather is cool and dry, then it gets hotter and hotter until the monsoon rains begin.

Northeast India and Bangladesh have even more rain than Bombay. But large areas of northwest India are desert.

Bombay monthly rainfall
700 millimetres
600
500
400
300
200
100
0
J F M A M J J A S O N D
Total annual rainfall 2078mm

SOUTHEAST ASIA

Scale 1:25 000 000

1 cm on the map = 250 km on the ground

1 inch on the map = 400 miles on the ground

Height of the land
- over 6000 metres
- 4000 - 6000
- 2000 - 4000
- 1000 - 2000
- 400 - 1000
- 200 - 400
- 0 - 200 metres
- below sea level

▲ Highest point on the map

Country boundaries
Large cities
Bangkok Capital cities underlined

COPYRIGHT: GEORGE PHILIP & SON. LTD.

120° East from Greenwich

Stamps from Southeast Asia.
Singapore *has four main religions:*

Christian church   Buddhist temple   Islamic mosque   Hindu temple

▶ **Laos.** *Elephants carry huge logs from the jungle. Laos was once called Lanxang – 'land of a million elephants'.*

Vietnam. *Children learn to draw their country. North and South Vietnam were united in 1976 after many years of fighting.*

The Equator crosses Southeast Asia, so it is always hot. Heavy tropical rainstorms are common, too.

The mainland and most of the islands are very mountainous. The mountains are covered with thick tropical forest (look at the stamp of Laos). These areas are very difficult to reach and have few people. The large rivers are important routes inland. Their valleys and deltas are very crowded indeed.

Indonesia is the biggest country. It used to be the Dutch East Indies.

The Philippines is another large group of islands, south of China. They were Spanish until 1898.

Malaysia includes part of the mainland and most of northern Borneo.

Singapore is an island at the tip of mainland Malaysia, but a separate country. Both countries were once British and Singapore still belongs to the Commonwealth.

Burma was part of the Indian Empire. It became independent in 1948.

Vietnam, Laos and **Cambodia** were once called French Indo-China. The full name of Laos is written in French on the stamp.

Thailand has always been independent, and has a king. It used to be called Siam.

Floating market in Thailand.
Farmers bring their fruit and vegetables to Bangkok market by boat. On some boats there are fish which are cooked on the boat and sold for lunch.
▼

▲
Harvesting rice. *Rice grows on terraces cut into the mountainside in Bali. Each terrace is sown and harvested by hand. Bali is a small island east of Java. Some people claim that it is the most beautiful island of Indonesia, and all the world!*

A Thai schoolbook. *This page from a children's book about Thailand shows a man harvesting pineapples. Can you see how he waters the fields from the river?*
▼

Fact box: Indonesia

Did you know that Indonesia: has the **fifth largest population** in the world (see page 9); is the **world's greatest archipelago** – a group of 13,000 islands, which stretches for 5600 kilometres; has **more active volcanoes** than any other country (77); suffered the **world's biggest recorded bang** – when the island of Krakatoa blew up in a volcanic eruption in 1883.

ประเทศ ไทย ของ ฉัน   มี ต้น ข้าว มี ต้น ผัก
และ มี ต้น ผลไม้ มาก มาย

In Thailand we have plenty of
rice, vegetables and fruit.

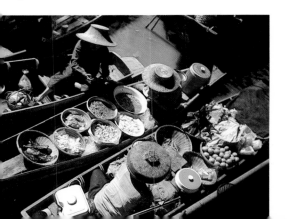

CHINA
AND NEIGHBOURS

U.S.S.R.

MONGOLIA

Ulan Bator

Dzungarian Desert

Urumchi

Tian Shan

Tarim

Takla Makan

Kunlun Shan

Nan Shan

C H I N A

Tibet

Himalayas

Tsangpo (Brahmaputra) Lhasa

Mount Everest 8848

INDIA

NEPAL

BHUTAN

BANGLA-DESH

BURMA

Mekong

Gobi

Great Khingan Mts.

Manchuria

Sungari

Tsitsihar

Harbin

U.S.S.R.

Changchun

Shenyang Fushun

Anshan

NORTH KOREA

Sea of Japan

Peking

Paotow

Tangshan

Pyongyang

Dalien

Seoul

SOUTH KOREA

Tientsin

Great Wall of China

Taiyuan

Tsinan

Taegu

Pusan

JAPAN

Yellow

Tsingtao

Sea

Lanchow

Hwang Ho

Chengchow

Sian

Nanking

Shanghai

Ryukyu

Wuhan

Yangtze

East

Is.

Chengtu

Chungking

Nanchang

China

Changsha

Foochow

Sea

Taipei

Tropic of Cancer

Kweiyang

Kweilin

TAIWAN

Kunming

Si Kiang

Canton

Kaohsiung

Macao (Port.)

HONG KONG (U.K.)

VIETNAM

South China

Sea

LAOS

Hainan

PHILIPPINES

Height of the land

▲ Highest point on the map

| over 6000 metres |
| 4000 - 6000 |
| 2000 - 4000 |
| 1000 - 2000 |
| 400 - 1000 |
| 200 - 400 |
| 0 - 200 metres |
| below sea level |

sea level

Country boundaries

◼ ◼ ● Large cities

Peking Capital cities underlined

Scale 1:25 000 000

0   200km   400km   600km   800km

1 cm on the map = 250 km on the ground

0   200miles   400miles   600miles

1 inch on the map = 400 miles on the ground

110° East from Greenwich

COPYRIGHT. GEORGE PHILIP & SON. LTD.

China's amazing mountains. *Both the stamp and the photograph show the amazing shapes of the limestone mountains in southern China. The mountains that look 'unreal' in Chinese paintings really are real! It is almost impossible to travel through this area except by boat. The heavy rain has slowly dissolved the limestone to make these picturesque mountains. They are now one of China's main tourist attractions. The river is the Kwei which flows through Kweilin, an old city dating back to the sixth century.*

48

China has over a billion people (1,000,000,000) – more than any other country in the world. The map shows that there are many high mountains in China, such as the huge plateau of Tibet and the rugged mountains of the southwest where the Giant Pandas live. Not many people live in these mountains, nor in the deserts of the north, near Mongolia. So the lower land of eastern China is *very* crowded indeed. Rice grows well south of the River Yangtze. North of the Yangtze, where the winters are colder, wheat and maize are important food crops, but it is hard to grow enough.

Building a reservoir. *Everybody, male and female, pulls a heavy cart of rocks to make a new dam across a river. The dam will provide water for power and for irrigation – and it will control flooding too. China has made great progress with projects like this, which use lots of people and few machines. Long ago the Great Wall of China was built in this way to keep out China's enemies.*

▼

China's neighbours

Mongolia is a huge desert country, three times bigger than Spain. It is the world's emptiest country: there are fewer than 2 million people.

North Korea is a communist country. It separated from South Korea in the Korean War in 1953.

South Korea has over 40 million people – more than Canada and Australia put together!

Taiwan is an island country which used to be called Formosa, or nationalist China. It is not communist and is not part of the rest of China.

Hong Kong will be a British colony until 1997, when the land will be handed back to China. Big new skyscrapers stand on the hills to fit 5 million people into a crowded island. The hydrofoil is going to **Macao**, a nearby Portuguese colony.

▼

◄ **Traffic in Tientsin.** *Rush hour in Chinese cities is not the same as in New York or London: there are hardly any cars. People travel on foot, or by bicycle or bus. Tientsin is a big port in northern China and is one of the largest cities in the country.*

Fact box

* One person out of every five people in the world is Chinese.

* This century's worst earthquake happened in Tangshan in 1976. This is in the crowded part of China, so many people were killed.

* The Chinese invented an earthquake detector 1800 years ago. They also invented the compass, paper and printing.

* The place furthest from the open sea is in China: the Dzungarian Desert, 2400 kilometres from the sea. A man from Norwich in England who cycled there said it is 'hot and horrible'!

* The highest plateau in the world is Tibet. Its average height is nearly 5000 metres above sea-level – as high as Mont Blanc (see page 27)! Lhasa, Tibet, has the world's highest airport, at 4363 metres. The runway is extra long as there is so little air pressure to help aircraft take off.

* The Chinese language has many dialects: the commonest is Mandarin. Each sound has four tones; words are written using thousands of different characters. Chinese used to be written from top to bottom of the page; now it is written from left to right.

JAPAN

Bullet train. *Japan's 'bullet trains' go like a bullet from a gun! The trains run on new tracks with no sharp curves to slow them down. They provide a superb service except when there is an earthquake warning. When that happens, the trains have to go more slowly, to be safe.*

Japan is quite a small country: it is smaller than France or Spain. Canada is twenty-seven times as big as Japan! But Japan has a big population – about 121,000,000. This is over twice as many people as France, and five times as many as Canada.

People talk of the 'Japanese miracle'. This small country is mostly mountains, has very few mines and hardly any oil, yet it has become the world's biggest producer of televisions, radios, music centres, cameras, trucks, ships and many other things. Japanese cars and computers are admired throughout the world. There are booming cities in the south of Japan, with highly skilled, hard-working people. But most of Japan is still peaceful and beautiful.

In the south rice is the main food crop. Some of the hillsides look like giant steps, because they are terraced to make flat fields for growing rice.

Mount Fuji in winter. *Fujiyama (Mount Fuji) is Japan's most famous mountain. It is an old volcano, 3776 metres high. In winter, the upper slopes are snow-covered. The 'bullet trains' pass Mount Fuji on their high-speed journey from Tokyo to Nagoya and Osaka.*

Huge baskets for live fish. *Fish are caught and then stored in these huge baskets. The Japanese eat more fish than people in any other country, but sadly the seas near Japan have been polluted by industry. Big Japanese trawlers now fish thousands of kilometres away from home.*

Many mountains are volcanoes. There are 54 active volcanoes, and over 100 others (see below). The northernmost island, Hokkaido, is much less crowded. It has very cold winters, and even the summers are too cold for growing rice.

Horyu Temple, at Nara

The beautiful temple on the right is called a pagoda. Japanese pagodas are carefully preserved. Their unusual shape originally came partly from Indian temples and partly from Chinese temples. This is one of many Japanese stamps on the theme of national treasures. You could collect them.

45°

U.S.S.R.

CHINA

Sea of Okhotsk

Wakkanai

La Perouse Str.

Kunashir Str.

Nemuro Str.

Asahigawa

HOKKAIDO

Otaru

Sapporo

Kushiro

NORTH KOREA

Hakodate

Tsugaru Strait

40°

Aomori

Hachinohe

SEA OF JAPAN

Akita

Kitakami

PACIFIC

Sendai

Sado

Niigata

Fukushima

SOUTH KOREA

OCEAN

Kanazawa

Toyama

Utsunomiya

Hitachi

Oki Is.

Tone

Tokyo

Yokohama

Kawasaki

Gifu

Korea Strait

Kyoto

Kiso

Nagoya

Mt. Fuji ▲ 3776

Tsushima

Kobe

Nara

Hamamatsu

Hiroshima

Okayama

Sakai

Osaka

Kitakyushu

Inland Sea

Matsuyama

SHIKOKU

Fukuoka

KYUSHU

Kumamoto

Nagasaki

Kagoshima

Tanega I.

Height of the land

over 6000 metres
4000 - 6000
2000 - 4000
1000 - 2000
400 - 1000
200 - 400
0 - 200 metres
below sea level

▲ Highest point on the map

sea level

Country boundaries
Large cities
Tokyo Capital city underlined

Scale 1: 7 500 000

0   75km   150km   225km   300km   375km   450km

1 cm on the map = 75 km on the ground

0   75miles   150miles   225miles   300miles

1 inch on the map = 120 miles on the ground

East from Greenwich

51

AFRICA

◀ **Children in Ghana.** *Everywhere in Africa, there are lots of children. The fathers of these children are fishermen: in the background you can see big dug-out canoes. The canoes are made from the huge trees of the rain-forest, and can cope with big waves in the Gulf of Guinea. These children get plenty of fish to eat, but in some parts of Africa hunger is a major problem.*

Most of the countries of Africa have quite small populations – except for Nigeria and Egypt. But everywhere the population is growing fast. It is difficult to provide enough schools and clinics for all the children and there are not enough good jobs. So African countries are trying hard to improve fishing, mining, and industry.

Fact box: Africa

Area 30,319,000 square kilometres

Highest point Mount Kilimanjaro (Tanzania), 5895 metres

Lowest point Shores of Lake Assal (Djibouti), 155 metres below sea-level

Longest river Nile, 6670 kilometres (also a *world* record)

Largest lake Lake Victoria (East Africa), 69,484 square kilometres

Biggest country Sudan, 2,505,813 square kilometres

Smallest country *Mainland:* Gambia, 11,295 square kilometres; *islands:* Seychelles, 308 square kilometres (see p. 9)

◀ **The pyramids of Egypt.** *The pyramids are tombs which were built by slaves over 4000 years ago. They are still the biggest buildings in the whole of Africa. They are near the River Nile, in the Sahara desert.*
These camels are for the tourists that visit the pyramids.

Imagine travelling southwards across Africa, along the 20°E line of longitude. You start in Libya. Your first 1000 kilometres will be across the great Sahara desert (where you *must* travel in winter) – sand, rock and the high rugged Tibesti Mountains. Then you reach thorn bushes, in the semi-desert Sahel area of Chad.

By 15°N you are into savanna – very long grass and scattered trees. You cross the country known as CAR for short. The land becomes greener and at about 5°N you reach the equatorial rain-forest . . . a real jungle! You are now in Zaïre.

Then the same story happens in reverse – savanna in Angola; then semi-desert (the Kalahari and the Karoo). Finally you reach the mountains and coast of South Africa – a journey of nearly 8000 kilometres.

Where do the country names come from?

Ghana, Benin, Mali
Names of great empires in West Africa a long time ago

Gambia, Niger, Nigeria
From big rivers in these countries

Chad From Lake Chad

Namibia From the *Namib* desert

Tanzania From *Tan*ganyika (the mainland) and the island of *Zan*zibar

Sierra Leone 'Lion Mountain' in Portuguese (named by explorers)

Ivory Coast Ivory, from the tusks of elephants, used to be traded along this coast

NORTH AFRICA

Most of North Africa is desert – but not all. The coastlines and mountains of northwest Africa get winter rain: good crops are grown, and the area is popular all year with tourists from Europe. These countries are Islamic. **Morocco** has the oldest university in the world: the Islamic University in Fez.

Oil has made **Libya** rich. The other countries still have much poverty. The Sahel states, at the southern edge of the Sahara, are among the poorest countries in the world. They had severe famines in the 1970s and 1980s.

Egypt has the biggest population of any North African country. Its capital, Cairo, is one of the biggest cities in the world. The River Nile brings water to the valley and delta. The land is carefully farmed (with irrigation) and crowded with people; the rest of Egypt is almost empty. The map shows that part of the desert is *below* sea-level.

The lack of rain has helped to preserve many of the marvellous monuments, palaces and tombs built by the ancient Egyptians. The pyramids at Giza, near Cairo, are 4500 years old (see page 53). They are the only one of the Seven Wonders of the ancient world still surviving.

◄**Oasis, Algeria.** *The water allows date-palms to grow well. But in the background, great sand-dunes loom on the skyline: if they advance, they may cover the oasis one day. In the foreground there is rock desert – that is more common than sand desert.*

Huge sand-dunes, Libya. *Land-Rover tracks can be seen in the foreground. But no vehicles can cross the huge, steep sand-dunes in the background. The Land-Rover has stopped in front of the dunes. Only about a tenth of the Sahara desert is made up of sand-dunes. Other parts are gravel desert, rock desert, salt desert, dried-up lakes, and desert mountains.*
▼

▲
Camels at market, Tunisia. *Camels are ideal for deserts: they can survive for a long time without water, by relying on the fat in their humps. They can carry heavy loads, and can walk well on soft sand. But nowadays, lorries are taking over from camels for long-distance travel.*

Puzzle picture

This is a satellite photograph of part of the Sahara desert in southern Libya. Who has drawn these circles in the desert, and why? How have they become green? Why are some circles more green than others?

Have a guess – then turn to page 96.

The Suez Canal. *This container ship is travelling through the desert of Egypt! The Suez Canal was dug in 1859–69 by Arabs, organized by a Frenchman, Ferdinand de Lesseps. Before the canal was dug, the route from Europe to India and the Far East was round the whole of Africa.*

For almost a century, the canal was a very important route; but now aeroplanes have taken over almost all the passenger traffic, and many oil-tankers are much too big to go through it. Today it is mostly used for freight travelling from Asia to Europe.

▼

Saharan records

The Sahara is the **biggest desert** in the world. It is over 8 million square kilometres in size. From west to east it is over 5000 kilometres; from north to south it extends about 2000 kilometres and it is still growing.

The **hottest shade temperature** ever recorded, 58°C, was in Al Aziziyah, Libya, in 1922.

The **sunniest** place in the world, over 4300 hours of sunshine per year, is in the eastern Sahara.

The **highest sand-dunes** in the world, 430 metres high, are in east central Algeria.

The **longest river** in the world is the River Nile, 6670 kilometres. (How strange that a desert should have the world's longest river!)

WEST AFRICA

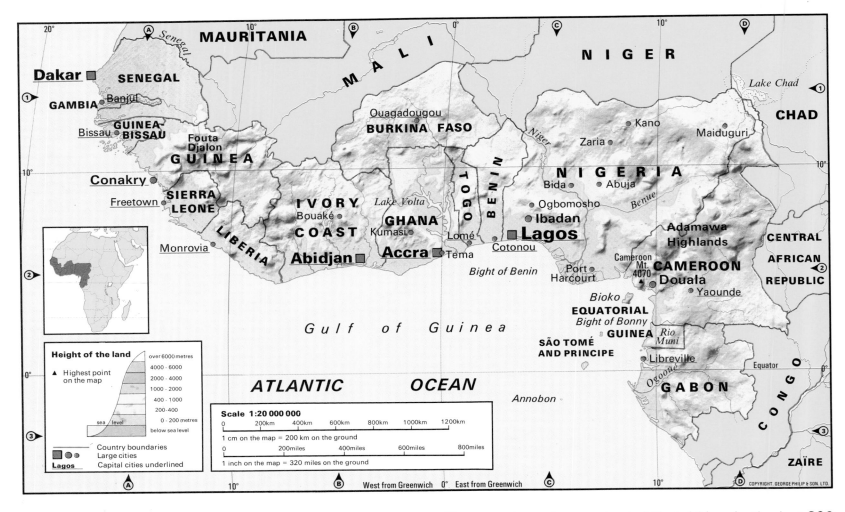

There are lots of countries in West Africa. In the last 300 years, European countries grabbed parts of the coastline and later they took over the inland areas as well. Now, all the countries are independent, but still use the language of those who once ruled them. English, French, Spanish or Portuguese is spoken. Many Africans speak a European language as well as one or more African languages. Nigeria is the largest and most important country in West Africa. It has over 100 million people – more than any other African country. Although English is the official language, there are about 240 others in Nigeria!

◄ **Market day.** *Red peppers for sale in Bida, Nigeria. Red peppers are very popular in West Africa – they give a strong flavour in cooking. Markets are important in both towns and villages in all the countries of West Africa. Most of the selling is done by women.*

56

Puzzle picture

Why is this man building all these mounds? Make a guess – then turn to page 96.

◄**Extinct volcanoes.** *Long ago these mountains in Cameroon were volcanoes. Now only the cores of the volcanoes are left: the rest has been eroded away. Notice the thatched roofs of the houses.*

Everywhere in West Africa there is rapid progress. Most children now go to primary school, and the capital cities have televisions and airports. But many people are still very poor.

The southern part of West Africa, near the Equator, is forested. The tall trees are being felled for their hardwood. Many crops are grown in the forest area and sold overseas: cocoa (for chocolate-making in England); coffee, pineapples and bananas (for export to France); rubber (for car and lorry tyres). The main food crops are root crops, such as cassava and yams.

Further north, the trees thin out and there is savanna. The tall grass with some trees is suitable for cattle farming. There are big herds of cattle, and beautiful leather goods are on sale in the markets. Cotton and groundnuts (peanuts) are grown in the

savanna lands. The main food crops are grass-like: rice, maize, sorghum and millet.

Yeji ferry, Ghana. *This big ferry carries lorries, cars, people and their heavy loads across Lake Volta. This man-made lake flooded Ghana's main road to the north. You can see trees that died as the water rose in the new lake.*

Harvesting rice in Ghana. *This view could be in Europe or North America! Huge combine-harvesters are reaping rice on a large farm in northern Ghana. But most farms are very small.* ▶

57

EAST AND CENTRAL AFRICA

Fishermen, Zaïre. *Each one of these fishing boats is made from a single tree, hollowed out with an axe. They are called dug-out canoes – there is no danger of a leak in the boat!*

Bus services in Africa

Bus journeys in Africa are exciting, and the fares are very cheap, but many roads are very bumpy!

'Safari' is the Swahili word for 'journey'. This bus ticket is for a journey (safari) in Tanzania from Moshi to Dar es Salaam.

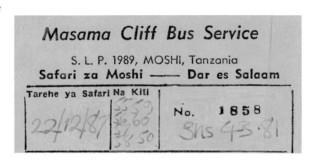

Masama Cliff Bus Service
S. L. P. 1989, MOSHI, Tanzania
Safari za Moshi ——— Dar es Salaam
Tarehe ya Safari Na Kiti
22/12/87
No. 1858
Shs 43.81

Picking tea in Nandi province, Kenya. *The tender young leaves are picked by hand and taken to a factory where they will be dried and crushed. Tea grows well in the highlands of East Africa. It is an important export of Kenya.*

Central Africa is mostly lowland, with magnificent trees in the tropical rain-forest in Zaïre and Congo. Some timber is used for buildings and canoes (see photograph above left); some is exported. The cleared land can grow many tropical crops.

East Africa is mostly high savanna land with long grass, and scattered trees. Small parts are reserved for wild animals (see opposite page); in other parts, there are large farms for export crops such as coffee and tea. But in most of East Africa, the people keep cattle and grow crops for their own needs.

The Somali Republic, Djibouti, northern Kenya, and northern Ethiopia are desert areas.

The Masai people *live mainly by herding cattle on the plains near the border of Kenya and Tanzania. These teenage boys are dressed as warriors. They learn to hunt and to guard the cattle. A Masai man has been Prime Minister of Tanzania.*

Ethiopia is largely mountainous. In most years there is plenty of rain, but this can bring floods and wash away the good soil. In 1985, the country had a terrible famine.

In all these countries the population is growing fast, there is much poverty, and people are moving to the cities. But there are also many signs of development: new farm projects, new ports and roads, and new schools.

58

Zebra and wildebeest at Ngorongoro, Tanzania. People come from all over the world to go on wildlife safaris in East Africa. This lake is in the crater of an old volcano. Animals gather to drink the water, because there is no other water nearby in the long dry season.

The game reserves of East Africa are carefully managed to conserve the wildlife. Elephants, lions, and giraffes are only 'shot' by cameras now: guns are banned. The money spent by tourists is very important for Kenya and Tanzania.

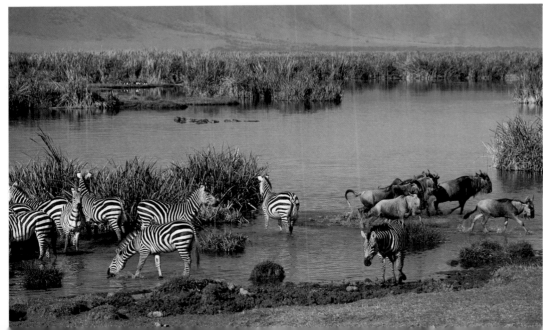

59

SOUTHERN AFRICA

Most of southern Africa is a high, flat plateau. The rivers cannot be used by ships because of big waterfalls like the Victoria Falls (see page 61). But the rivers can be useful. Two huge dams have been built on the River Zambezi – at Kariba (in Zambia) and at Cahora Bassa (in Mozambique). The map shows the lakes behind each dam. The power of the falling water is used to make electricity.

Angola and **Mozambique** used to be Portuguese colonies, and Portuguese is still their official language – though many different African languages are spoken, too. Most of the other countries shown on the map have English as their official language.

Notice that many southern African countries are land-locked: they have no coastline. The railways leading to the ports in neighbouring countries are very important. Copper from Zambia and Botswana and asbestos from Zimbabwe are sent abroad in this way.

The **Republic of South Africa** is the wealthiest country in Africa. It has the richest gold-mine in the world, and also priceless diamond-mines. But most of the black people are very poor. They have been kept apart from the white people by the government, which is run by white people. This policy is called apartheid.

All the other countries of southern Africa disagree with apartheid – even Lesotho, a country which is completely surrounded by South Africa. Some parts of South Africa have been made into Bantustans – mini-countries which are partly run by Africans. But they are not recognized as real countries by the United Nations, so they are not on our map.

A village in Zambia

Sianga drew this picture of her village during a lesson at her school in Zambia. Her village is close to the River Zambezi in the west of the country.

An unfriendly notice *in three languages on a white-owned poultry farm in South Africa.*

A baobab tree. *In almost all southern Africa there is a long, hot dry season. The baobab tree is good at surviving a long drought. It has a specially fat trunk and main branches which hold water like a sponge and help to keep it alive.*

World Greats

The **Victoria Falls** (*right*) are on the River Zambezi, at the border of Zambia and Zimbabwe. Africans call the falls *Mosi-oi-tunya* – 'the smoke that thunders'. They were named after the English Queen Victoria by the explorer David Livingstone.
The world's **oldest mines** are in Swaziland. Iron ore was mined here 43,000 years ago.
The world's **deepest mine** is the gold-mine at Carletonville, South Africa. It is 3777 metres deep – and still getting deeper!

The world's **biggest diamond** was found near Pretoria, South Africa, in 1905.
Mining diamonds. *Diamonds are mined in several countries in southern Africa. The huge mine shown here* (above right) *is in*

Namibia. The desert is scraped away to reach the rock beneath, where diamonds are found. The yellow lorry is huge, but looks very small in this vast mine.

Scale 1:20 000 000

| 0 | 200km | 400km | 600km | 800km | 1000km |

1 cm on the map = 200 km on the ground

| 0 | 200miles | 400miles | 600miles |

1 inch on the map = 320 miles on the ground.

Height of the land

- over 6000 metres
- 4000 – 6000
- 2000 – 4000
- 1000 – 2000
- 400 – 1000
- 200 – 400
- 0 – 200 metres
- below sea level

▲ Highest point on the map

Country boundaries
Large cities
Pretoria Capital cities underlined

COPYRIGHT. GEORGE PHILIP & SON. LTD.

NORTH AMERICA

North America includes many Arctic islands, a huge mainland area (quite narrow in Central America) and the islands in the Caribbean Sea. The map shows the great mountain ranges which are the most impressive feature of this continent. Almost all the west is mountainous; these are mostly fold mountains but the highest peaks are volcanoes. The Appalachian Mountains in the east are also fold mountains. And the island chains of the northwest (the Aleutian Islands) and the southeast (the West Indies) are the tops of underwater ranges.

Fruit market, Barbados, West Indies. *The West Indies have hot sunshine and plenty of rain. This is an ideal climate for growing excellent fruit. Which types of fruit can you recognize in this market? (Answer on page 96.)*

Height of the land

over 6000 metres	
4000 - 6000	
2000 - 4000	
1000 - 2000	
400 - 1000	
200 - 400	
sea level	0 - 200 metres
	below sea level

Deeper blue - deeper sea
▲ Highest point on the map

Scale 1: 50 000 000

0   500km   1000km   1500km   2000km   2500km

1 cm on the map = 500 km on the ground

0   500miles   1000miles   1500miles

1 inch on the map = 800 miles on the ground

The political map of North America is quite a simple one. The boundary between Canada and the USA is mostly at exactly 49°N. Four of the five Great Lakes have one shore in Canada and one shore in the USA.* Canada's two biggest cities, Toronto and Montreal, are south of the 49° line! Find them on the map on page 65.

The eight countries of Central America have more complicated boundaries. Six of these countries have two coastlines. The map shows that one country has a coastline only on the Pacific Ocean, and one has a coastline only on the Caribbean Sea.* The West Indies are made up of islands and there are lots of countries too. They are shown in more detail on pages 74 and 75.

Greenland was a colony of Denmark until quite recently, but now it is self-governing. Most of Greenland is covered by ice all year.

*Which ones? Answers on page 96.

Find them on the map on page 65.
They are shown in more detail on pages 74 and 75.
*Which ones? Answers on page 96.

Fact box: North America

Area 24,249,000 square kilometres
Highest point Mount McKinley (Alaska), 6194 metres
Lowest point Death Valley (California), 86 metres below sea-level
Longest river Red Rock-Missouri-Mississippi, 5970 kilometres
Largest lake Lake Superior*, 82,350 square kilometres
Biggest country Canada, 9,976,140 square kilometres
Smallest country Grenada (West Indies), 344 square kilometres
Richest country USA
Poorest country Haiti
Most crowded country Barbados
Least crowded country Canada

*The world's largest *fresh-water* lake

Flyovers, Los Angeles, USA.
There are four levels of road at this road junction in Los Angeles, yet there is a traffic-jam as well! The USA has more cars than any other country.

CANADA

Coin and flag. *Both the 1 cent coin and the flag show the national emblem of Canada, the maple leaf. In summer, the leaves of the maple tree are green, but in the fall (autumn) the leaves turn bright red. Canada's woodlands are specially beautiful in September and October (see photograph below right).*

Canadian Contrasts

This stamp is an air-picture of the prairies of central Canada. The huge flat fields of grain reach to the far horizon, and beyond. The only big buildings are grain elevators, for storing the harvested wheat.

In western Canada, the Rocky Mountains are high and jagged. There are glaciers among the peaks.

Only one country in the world is bigger than Canada*, but thirty countries have more people than Canada. Most of Canada is almost empty: very few people live on the islands of the north, or in the Northwest Territories, or in the western mountains, or near Hudson Bay. The farmland of the prairies (see the stamp) is uncrowded too. So . . . where *do* Canadians live?

The answer is that more Canadians live in cities than in the countryside. The map shows where the biggest cities are – all of them are in the southern part of Canada, and none are as far north as Norway or Sweden in Europe.

The photographs and stamps show Canada in summer. In winter, it is very cold indeed in central and northern Canada. Children go to school even when it is 40° below zero.

*Which country? See pages 38–9.

The Niagara Falls *are between Lake Erie and Lake Ontario, on the border of the USA and Canada. The tourists on the boat may get soaked by the spray! Big ships have to use a canal, with locks, to get past the falls.*

Languages in Canada

Canada has two official languages: French and English. So the stamps say 'Postes/Postage', instead of only 'Postage'. Most French-speaking Canadians live in the province of Quebec.

The biggest city in Quebec is Montreal: it is four times as big as Ottawa, the capital of Canada.

A long-distance train, *with diesel engines and silver coaches, crosses a viaduct in the province of Ontario. It is 4590 kilometres from Montreal to Vancouver by train. A hundred years ago it was the trans-Canada railway that helped to unite Canada as one country.*

How to remember the five Great Lakes

Try using the first letters of the Great Lakes to make a sentence:

Superior	Super
Michigan	Man
Huron	Helps
Erie	Every
Ontario	One

Now you'll *never* forget the west-to-east order of the Great Lakes!

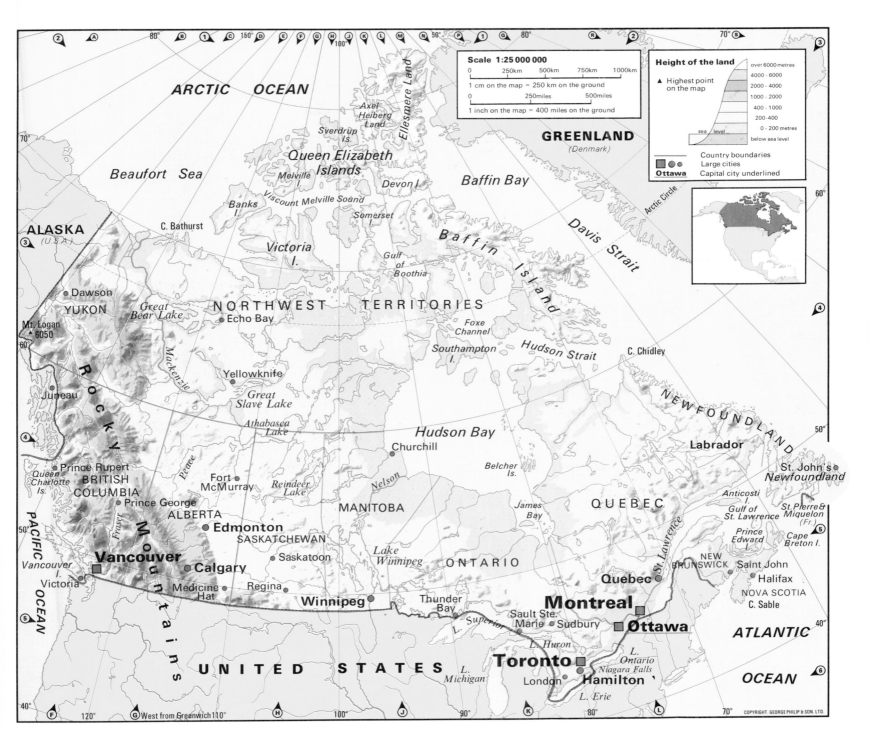

ARCTIC OCEAN

Axel Heiberg Land

Sverdrup Is.

Ellesmere Land

GREENLAND
(Denmark)

Queen Elizabeth Islands

Melville I.

Devon I.

Baffin Bay

Banks I.

Viscount Melville Sound

Somerset I.

Arctic Circle

Davis Strait

Beaufort Sea

C. Bathurst

ALASKA
(U.S.A.)

Victoria I.

Gulf of Boothia

Baffin Island

Dawson

YUKON

Great Bear Lake

Echo Bay

NORTHWEST   TERRITORIES

Foxe Channel

C. Chidley

Mt. Logan 6050

Juneau

Mackenzie

Yellowknife

Great Slave Lake

Athabasca Lake

Hudson Strait

Southampton I.

Hudson Bay

Churchill

Belcher Is.

Labrador

NEWFOUNDLAND

St. John's Newfoundland

Prince Rupert

Queen Charlotte Is.

BRITISH COLUMBIA

Prince George

Fort McMurray

Reindeer Lake

Peace

Nelson

MANITOBA

James Bay

QUEBEC

Anticosti I.

Gulf of St. Lawrence

St.Pierre & Miquelon (Fr.)

ALBERTA

Edmonton

SASKATCHEWAN

Lake Winnipeg

ONTARIO

Prince Edward I.

Cape Breton I.

PACIFIC OCEAN

Vancouver I.

Vancouver

Victoria

Fraser

Calgary

Saskatoon

Medicine Hat

Regina

Winnipeg

Thunder Bay

L. Superior

Sault Ste. Marie

Sudbury

St. Lawrence

Quebec

NEW BRUNSWICK

Saint John

Halifax

NOVA SCOTIA

C. Sable

Montreal

Ottawa

ATLANTIC

L. Huron

L. Michigan

Toronto

London

Hamilton

L. Ontario

Niagara Falls

L. Erie

OCEAN

UNITED   STATES

West from Greenwich

COPYRIGHT. GEORGE PHILIP & SON. LTD.

◀ **Montreal: old and new.** *The old houses have been pulled down, to make way for huge new office blocks. Three million people live in Montreal.*

The St Lawrence. *This big ship is passing islands in the St Lawrence river. The ship is going from the Great Lakes to the Atlantic Ocean. A seaway with huge locks has been built to bypass the rapids, shallows and waterfalls on parts of the river.* ▶

USA

Alaska is the biggest state of the USA – but it has the fewest people. It was bought from Russia in 1867 for seven million dollars: the best bargain ever, particularly as oil was discovered a hundred years later. Oil has helped Alaska to become rich. Fish and timber are the other main products. Much of Alaska is mountainous or covered in forest. In the north, there is darkness all day in December, and months of ice-cold weather.

Flag of Alaska. *The flag of Alaska shows stars in the northern sky known as the 'plough' or 'the big dipper'. At the top right is the Pole Star: this reminds us that Alaska is in the far north. The flag was chosen in a competition; the winner was only 13 years old.*

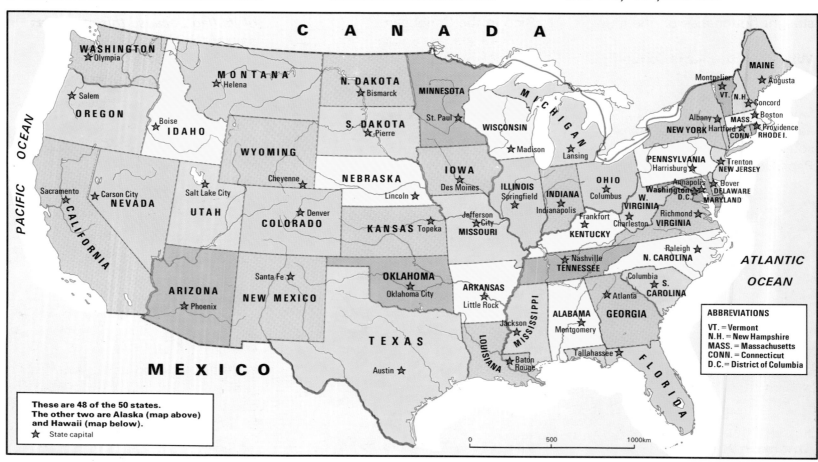

These are 48 of the 50 states. The other two are Alaska (map above) and Hawaii (map below).
☆ State capital

ABBREVIATIONS
VT. = Vermont
N.H. = New Hampshire
MASS. = Massachusetts
CONN. = Connecticut
D.C. = District of Columbia

Hawaii *is the newest state in the USA: it became a state in 1959. Honolulu is on Oahu island.*

These faraway Pacific islands are the tops of volcanoes, over 3000 kilometres from mainland USA (see the map on page 83). If the height of Mauna Kea is measured from the sea-bed, it is 10,023 metres, the tallest mountain in the world.

Stars and stripes

In 1776 there were only 13 states in the USA; so the US flag had 13 stars and 13 stripes. As more and more states joined the USA, more stars were added to the flag. Now there are 50 states, and 50 stars. But the 13 stripes on today's flag still recall the original 13 states.

The maps show the 50 states of the USA. The first 13 states were all on the east coast: these states were settled by Europeans who had sailed across the Atlantic (see the photograph of a pilgrim ship on page 69).

As the Americans moved westward, so more and more states were formed. The western states are bigger than the states in the east. You can see their straight boundaries on the map.

Who are 'the Americans'?

Out of every 100 people in the USA, 83 have ancestors from Europe. Colonists came from Britain to the eastern states, from France to the southern states, and from Spain to the Pacific coastline in the west. Later on,

people came from almost all parts of Europe to the USA. About 12 people out of every 100 came from West Africa, brought to the USA as slaves to work in the southern states. By 1865, the slaves were free. Many black Americans now live in the northeast USA. More recently, many Spanish-speaking people have entered the USA from Mexico and from Puerto Rico in the Caribbean.

There are fewer than one million American Indians now, some of whom live on special 'reservations'.

5 cent coin. E PLURIBUS UNUM *on this coin is Latin for 'Out of many – one': many peoples have come together to become one country. This 5 cent piece is called a nickel.*

State flags. *Each state has its own flag and some of them tell you about the history of the state.*

Wyoming *has a buffalo in the centre of its flag because this state was part of the Wild West where buffaloes used to roam freely.*

Mississippi *has the French flag (red, white and blue stripes) because it belonged to France until 1803.*

The cross at top left was used as a flag by the southern states in the Civil War in 1861–5.

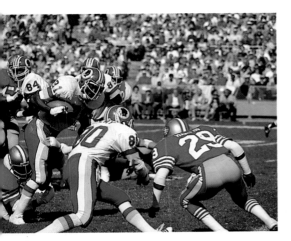

American football. *The Washington Redskins play the San Francisco 49ers. The team from the west coast has travelled 4500 kilometres for this game. The players travel by air – it takes three days to cross the USA by train!*

	New York	Miami	Chicago	New Orleans	Seattle
Miami	2138				
Chicago	1346	2198			
New Orleans	2131	1406	1488		
Seattle	4613	5445	3288	4211	
San Francisco	4850	4915	3499	3622	1352

Road distances in kilometres

Distance chart

Read the chart just like a tables-chart, or a graph. The distance chart shows how big the USA is. In fact, New York is nearer to London, England, than it is to San Francisco! How far is it from Seattle to Miami? New Orleans to Chicago? (Find these places on the maps on pages 68–71). (Answers on page 96.)

EASTERN USA

Which US city is most important?

Washington is the capital city, where the President lives. But *New York* has far more people and industries than Washington. So *both* are the most important city – but in different ways.

The map shows only half the USA, but over three-quarters of the population live in this half of the country.

The great cities of the northeast were the first big industrial areas in America. Pittsburgh's American football team is still called the Pittsburgh Steelers, even though many of the steel-works have closed down.

In recent years, many people have moved from the 'snow-belt' of the north to the 'sun-belt' of the south. New industries are booming in the south, where once there was much poverty. And many older people retire to Florida, where even midwinter feels almost like summer.

The Appalachian Mountains are beautiful, especially in the fall (autumn), when the leaves of the trees turn red. But this area is the poorest part of the USA. Coal-mines have closed and farmland is poor. The good farmland is west of the Appalachians, where you can drive for hundreds of kilometres past wheat and sweetcorn. In the south it is hot enough for cotton, tobacco and peanuts to be successful crops.

Plan for better cities!

Turn the book clockwise and you will see patios, parks and gardens among the skyscrapers!

Washington, DC. *There is a world of difference between the well-kept rich suburbs* (above) *and the run-down slum area* (right) *of Washington, DC, the capital city of the USA.*

Manhattan Island, New York. *The world's first skyscrapers were built on Manhattan Island: the hard granite rock gave good foundations. The older skyscrapers each have a different shape; the newer ones are flat-topped.*

▲

Plantation-owner's house in Virginia. *Plantation owners grew rich from tobacco and cotton. They lived in fine houses like this one. But their slaves lived in very poor houses.*

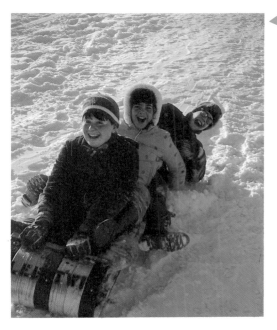

◄ **Winter in Pittsburgh.** *Winter in the northern USA can be very cold indeed. But these Pittsburgh children are enjoying the fresh, crisp snow, before it becomes polluted by smoke from the steel-works and factories.*

The Earth from the Moon

This is the view that American astronauts saw from the Moon. Half the Earth is in darkness. Neil Armstrong of the USA was the first man on the Moon, 21 July 1969.

▲

Pilgrim ship, New England. *The Pilgrim Fathers sailed to America in 1620 from England to start a new life. In 1957 a replica pilgrim ship was built and sailed to America.*

Puzzle stamp

Which river is this? Where does it flow to? And why is it called 'Great River Road'? (Answer on page 96.)

Map

Scale 1:20 000 000

0   200km   400km   600km   800km

1 cm on the map = 200 km on the ground

0   200miles   400miles

1 inch on the map = 320 miles on the ground

Height of the land

▲ Highest point on the map

over 6000 metres
4000 - 6000
2000 - 4000
1000 - 2000
400 - 1000
200 - 400
sea level   0 - 200 metres
below sea level

—— Country boundaries
■ ● ● Large cities
Washington Capital city underlined
For the states of the U.S.A. see page 66

CANADA

Great Plains

Fargo
Duluth
Lake Superior
Minneapolis
St. Paul
Green Bay
Sioux Falls
Mississippi
L. Michigan
Milwaukee
Detroit
Lake Huron
L. Ontario
Albany
Boston
C. Cod
Providence
Buffalo
Lake Erie
Chicago
Toledo
Cleveland
New York
Omaha
Missouri
Indianapolis
Columbus
Pittsburgh
Philadelphia
Baltimore
Washington
Kansas City
Cincinnati
Ohio
Richmond
St. Louis
Wichita
Louisville
Norfolk
Appalachian Mts.
Tulsa
Nashville
Tennessee
Blue Ridge
Mt. Mitchell 2037
Charlotte
ATLANTIC
Oklahoma City
Arkansas
Memphis
Mississippi
Chattanooga
Atlanta
Charleston
OCEAN
Red
Birmingham
Fort Worth
Dallas
Montgomery
Austin
Baton Rouge
Jacksonville
30°
Houston
New Orleans
C. Canaveral
San Antonio
Tampa
Palm Beach
Everglades
CLEAR WATER
BAHAMAS
Gulf of Mexico
Miami
C. Sable
West from Greenwich   90°   Key West   80°   COPYRIGHT, GEORGE PHILIP & SON. LTD.

WESTERN USA

Grand Canyon, Arizona. *The Colorado river has cut a huge canyon a mile deep in this desert area of the USA. The mountains slowly rose, while the river kept digging its valley deeper.*

Wheat harvest, USA. *Three huge combine harvesters move across a field of wheat. 150 years ago, this land was covered in grass and grazed by buffaloes. Much of this wheat will go abroad.*

American football

Many of the team names have a meaning that is linked to their city's geography or history.

San Francisco 49ers 1849 was the year of the great Californian Gold Rush, when many people came to look for gold.

Denver Broncos Denver, Colorado, was a centre for cowboys in the days of the Wild West: 'bucking broncos' were their horses!

Houston Oilers Houston, Texas, became a very wealthy city after oil was discovered.

Seattle Seahawks Seattle, Washington State, is on an inlet of the Pacific Ocean.

Do you know any other teams?

Rodeo in Montana. *There are few real cowboys nowadays – and trucks are used more than horses. But rodeos are popular with local people – and with tourists. At this junior rodeo at Big Timber, Montana, a young rider is trying to show his skill.*

California

California now has more people in it than any other state in the USA. It has every advantage. In the Central Valley the climate is right for many crops: oranges from California are well-known in the USA and abroad. Grapes grow well, and are made into wine.

The desert of the south is attractive to retired people – many people migrate here from all over the USA.

Many areas on this map have hardly any people. The Rocky Mountains are beautiful for holidays, but it is hard to make a living there. The only big city on the high plateaus west of the Rockies is Salt Lake City, Utah. Some former mining towns are now 'ghost towns': when the mines closed, all the people left. The toughest area of all is the desert land of Arizona in the southwest. The mountains and deserts were a great problem to the pioneers.

East of the Rockies are the Great Plains. The dry plains have enormous cattle ranches; where there is enough rain, crops of wheat and sweetcorn (maize) stretch to the horizon.

The Pacific coastlands of the northwest have plenty of rain and forestry is important. The climate is quite like northwest Europe.

What do the names mean?

The Spanish were the first settlers in the western USA, and they have left us many Spanish names. Here are some:

Amarillo (Texas) ..Yellow
Colorado ....Coloured
El Paso
 (Texas).................The pass
Los Angeles ....The angels
Las Vegas ....The fertile
 (Nevada)   plains
San José...............St Joseph
San Francisco .....St Francis
Sierra Nevada .....Snowy
                        Mountains

Street-car, San Francisco. ▶
Street-cars still climb the steep hills in San Francisco, California. A moving cable runs beneath the street. The car is fixed to the cable and starts with a jerk! There is a modern 'rapid transit' railway system too – but tourists prefer to see the city from the street-cars.

CENTRAL AMERICA

◀ **Ruins at Chichen Itza, Mexico.**
Great temples were built by the people known as Mayas over a thousand years ago. These amazing ruins are in Yucatan, the most easterly part of Mexico. Today, this is an area of jungle, with few people.

Something to cook

MEXICAN MAIZE TORTILLAS
Ingredients
225 grams of maize flour
(sweetcorn flour)
salt
water

Method
1 Mix the maize flour, salt, and water into a soft dough.
2 Pat into round shapes about $\frac{1}{2}$ centimetre thick, and 12 centimetres across.
3 Melt a little margarine in a frying-pan.
4 Place the tortillas in the hot frying-pan.
5 For best results, turn the tortillas over.
6 Serve at once!

You have now cooked one of the most important meals of Central America. Maize (sweetcorn) was developed as a crop in the Americas, and is now grown in many parts of the world. You eat maize often as Corn Flakes and semolina.

The Panama Canal *links the Caribbean Sea with the Pacific Ocean. It was opened in 1914. Many workers died of fever while digging the canal through the jungle. It is 82 kilometres long, and the deepest cutting is 82 metres deep – the world's biggest 'ditch'!*
There are six locks along the route of the canal. The photograph (below left) shows three ships in Gatun Lake, 26 metres above sea-level (see map). Over 15,000 ships use the canal each year, and sometimes there are 'traffic jams' at the locks: it is the busiest big ship canal in the world. Before the Panama Canal was built, the only sea route from Pacific to Atlantic
◀ *was round South America.*

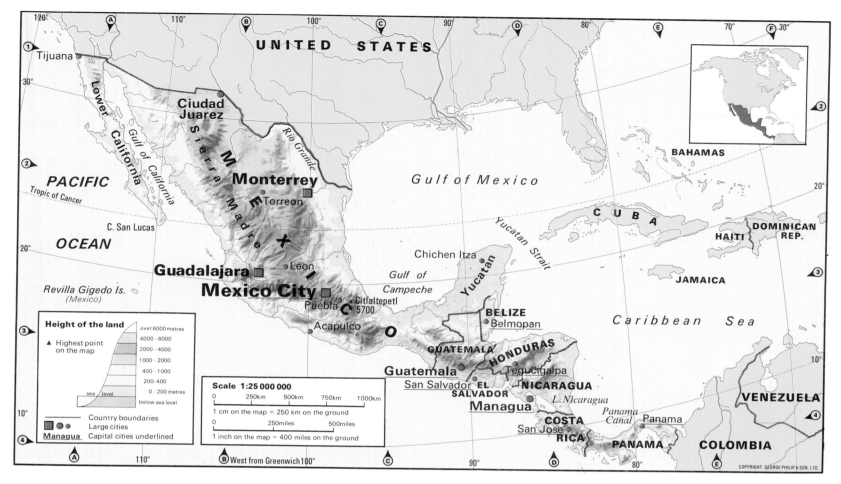

Mexico is by far the most important country on this map. Over 82 million people live in Mexico – more than in any country in Europe. Mexico City has a population of about 15 million: it is one of the biggest cities in the world. A major earthquake did much damage there in 1985.

Most Mexicans live on the high plateau of central Mexico. There are very few people in the northern desert, in Lower California in the northwest, in the southern jungle, or in Yucatan in the east.

The other seven countries on this map are quite small. None of them has as many people as Mexico City!

Once ruled by Spain, these countries have been independent since the 1820s. Revolutions and civil wars have caused many problems in Central America. But the climate is good for growing many tropical crops – once the jungle has been cleared.

What do the names mean?

Many names in the countries of Central America are based on Spanish, the official language.

El Salvador The Saviour (Jesus Christ)
San José (capital of Costa Rica) St Joseph
Costa Rica The rich coast
Pacific Ocean Peaceful ocean

Guatemala: drying coffee-beans. *Coffee berries grow on bushes in tropical countries. The berries are picked, and the seeds taken out and dried in the sun. We call these dried seeds coffee-beans.*

The man in the photograph is turning the beans, so that they dry on both sides.

Coffee is the most important export of several Central American countries. Many other tropical crops are exported, including sugar, bananas and pineapple.

▼

WEST INDIES

Scale 1:15 000 000

| 0 | 150km | 300km | 450km | 600km | 750km |

1 cm on the map = 150 km on the ground

| 0 | 150miles | 300miles | 450miles |

1 inch on the map = 240 miles on the ground

Height of the land

| over 6000 metres |
| 4000 - 6000 |
| 2000 - 4000 |
| 1000 - 2000 |
| 400 - 1000 |
| 200 - 400 |
| 0 - 200 metres |
| below sea level |

▲ Highest point on the map

sea level

Country boundaries
Large cities
Capital cities underlined

Havana

U.S.A.

Grand Bahama

Freeport

Gulf of Mexico

Nassau *Eleuthera I.*

BAHAMAS

Tropic of Cancer

A T L A N T I C   O C E A N

Florida Strait

25°

<u>Havana</u>

C U B A

Yucatan Strait

Camaguey

Caicos I. (U.K.)

Turks Is. (U.K.)

20°

Santiago de Cuba

Grand Cayman (U.K.)

G r e a t e r

Hispaniola

Santiago

HAITI **DOMINICAN REP.**

Pico Duarte ▲3175

San Juan

Virgin Is. (U.K.)

Anguilla

ST. CHRISTOPHER-NEVIS

ANTIGUA & BARBUDA

Montego Bay

JAMAICA

<u>Kingston</u>

A n t i l l e s

<u>Port-au-Prince</u>

<u>Santo Domingo</u>

PUERTO RICO (U.S.A.)

Montserrat

Guadeloupe (Fr.)

DOMINICA

15°

HONDURAS

C A R I B B E A N   S E A

L e s s e r A n t i l l e s

Martinique (Fr.)

ST. LUCIA

BARBADOS

ST. VINCENT & THE GRENADINES

<u>Bridgetown</u>

GRENADA

NICARAGUA

Aruba

Curaçao (Neth.)

Margarita

<u>Port of Spain</u>

TRINIDAD & TOBAGO

10°

COLOMBIA

V E N E Z U E L A

85° West from Greenwich

COPYRIGHT. GEORGE PHILIP & SON. LTD.

Farming in Jamaica

This one stamp shows the four most important farming exports of the West Indies.

Bananas (notice that they grow *upwards*!)

Citrus fruit (limes, grapefruit, oranges, lemons; with flowers and fruit at the same time!)

Sugar-cane (a giant grass-like crop; sugar comes from the sap)

Tobacco (made from the dried leaves)

The West Indies are a large group of islands in the Caribbean Sea. Some islands are high and volcanic, others are low coral islands – but all of them are beautiful. Most West Indians have African ancestors: they were brought from West Africa as slaves, to work in the sugar and tobacco fields.

Today, most of the islands are independent countries – and tourism is more important than farming in many places. Winter is the best time to visit; summer is very hot and humid, with the risk of hurricanes. In recent years many West Indians have emigrated to the UK from Commonwealth islands, to France from Guadeloupe and Martinique, and to the USA from Puerto Rico. A few islands have developed their minerals, for example bauxite in Jamaica and oil in Trinidad.

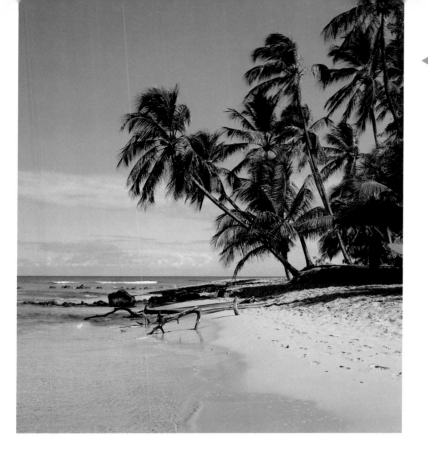

◄ **Coconut-palms and beach, Barbados.** *It is beautiful – but beware! The tropical sun can quickly burn your skin. And if you seek shade under the coconut-palms, you might get hit by a big coconut! Even so, the West Indies are very popular with tourists – especially Americans escaping from cold winters.*

▲

Loading bananas, Dominica. *Bananas are the main export of several islands. Here women are carrying heavy loads of bananas on their heads to the small boats which take the bananas to the Geest banana ship. The bananas travel to Europe in this refrigerated ship. Loading the ship is easier where islands have deep-water harbours.*

Dutch colonial houses, Curaçao. *The island of Curaçao has been Dutch for many years. The colonists came from the Netherlands, and tried to build houses just like the ones at home. Several other small West Indian islands still have European connections.*

▼

West Indian variety

In **Cuba**, Spanish is the main language. But Cuba is allied with the USSR, not with Spain: it has a communist ◄ government.

St Vincent is part of the Commonwealth and seems very British (but arrowroot and breadfruit only ► grow in the tropics).

Guadeloupe is not just French – it is officially part of France. This stamp was used in Guadeloupe *and* in ◄ all of France!

Curaçao is Dutch: the stamp shows Dutch colonial houses, and the Queen of the Netherlands. Compare the photograph (*right*). ►

◀ **Brasilia, Brazil.** *Brasilia became the new capital of Brazil in 1960. The photograph shows the parliament building on the left, built in concrete and shaped like a bowl, and a tall office block. Most Brazilians live near the coast, and Brasilia was a brave attempt to get people to move inland: it is 1000 kilometres from the sea. Over a million people now live there.*

Fact box: South America

Area 17,600,000 square kilometres

Highest point Mount Aconcagua (Argentina), 6960 metres

Lowest point No land below sea-level

Longest river Amazon, 6448 kilometres

Largest lake Lake Titicaca (Bolivia and Peru), 8285 square kilometres

Biggest country Brazil, 8,511,965 square kilometres

Smallest country Surinam*, 163,265 square kilometres

Richest country Venezuela

Poorest country Bolivia

Most crowded country Ecuador

Least crowded country Surinam

*French Guiana is smaller, but it is not independent

Reed-boat on Lake Titicaca.
Lake Titicaca is the highest navigable lake in the world: 3811 metres above sea-level. The fishing-boat is made of totora reeds which grow around the shores. Bundles of reeds are tied together, and even the sails are made of woven reeds.

The lake is shared between Peru and Bolivia. A steam-powered ferry-boat travels the length of the lake. A river flows southwards from Lake Titicaca to Lake Poopo, and then flows onwards and vanishes in the high, dry plateau.

Why is Lake Titicaca the only stretch of water available to the Bolivian navy? (Check the map.)

A tour of South America would be very exciting. At the Equator are the hot steamy jungles of the Amazon lowlands. To the west comes the great climb up to the Andes mountains. The peaks are so high that even the volcanoes are snow-capped all year. Travellers on buses and trains are offered extra oxygen to breathe, because the air is so thin.

Squeezed between the Andes and the Pacific Ocean in Peru and northern Chile is the world's driest desert. Further south in Chile are more wet forests — but these forests are cool. The Chilean pine (monkey-puzzle tree) originates here. But eastwards, in Argentina, there is less rain and more grass. Cattle on the Pampas are rounded up by cowboys, and further south is the very cold and dry area called Patagonia.

South America stretches further south than any other continent (apart from Antarctica). The cold and stormy tip of South America, Cape Horn, is only 1000 kilometres from Antarctica.

In every South American country, the population is growing fast. Most of the farmland is owned by a few rich people, and many people are desperately poor. Young people are leaving the countryside for the cities, most of which are encircled by shanty towns.

TROPICAL SOUTH AMERICA

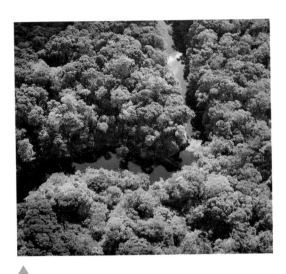

Amazon jungle *at the border of Guyana and Brazil. The hot, wet jungle covers thousands of kilometres. There is no cool season, and the forest is always green. The trees can be 50 metres high. New roads and villages, mines and dams are being built in the Brazilian jungle.*

The Andean states. Colombia, Ecuador, Peru and Bolivia are known as the Andean states. **Colombia** is known for its coffee. Bananas and other tropical crops grow near the coast of **Ecuador**, but the capital city is high in the mountains. **Peru** relies on mountain rivers to bring water to the dry coastal area.

Bolivia has the highest capital city in the world. It is the poorest country in South America: farming is difficult and even the tin-mines hardly make a profit.

East of the Andes, brave settlers are clearing parts of the forest.

Machu Picchu, Peru, *the lost city of the Incas, is perched on a mountainside 2400 metres above sea-level. The last Inca emperor probably lived here in 1580. The ruins were rediscovered in 1911.*

Brazil – the giant. Brazil is by far the biggest country in South America, and has more people than the rest of South America put together (about 140 million).

Most people still live near the coast. Parts of the Amazon forest are now being settled, but large areas inland are still almost empty. The poorest parts are in the northeast, where the rains often fail, and in the shanty towns around the big cities. Modern industry is growing very fast, but there are still too few jobs. Brazil has pioneered fuel made from sugar-cane for cars and trucks.

The llama *is the most important animal in the Andes – it provides milk, meat and leather for these Quechua Indian women. They are following one of the Inca tracks which linked the ancient cities.*

Caribbean Sea
Curaçao (Netherlands)

NICARAGUA

COSTA RICA

PANAMA
Gulf of Panama

Barranquilla
Gulf of Darien
Maracaibo
Medellin

Caracas
Barquisimeto
VENEZUELA
Bucaramanga

TRINIDAD & TOBAGO
Port of Spain

ATLANTIC

Bogota
Cali
COLOMBIA

Orinoco

Georgetown
Paramaribo
GUYANA
Cayenne
SURINAM
FRENCH GUIANA

OCEAN

Quito
ECUADOR

Negro

Galapagos Is. (Ecuador)

Guayaquil
Gulf of Guayaquil

Iquitos

Manaus
Amazon
Amazon

Belem

PERU

Madeira

Tapajos

Fortaleza

Trujillo

Huascaran
6768

São Francisco

Recife

Callao
Lima
Machu Picchu
Cuzco
Titicaca Lake

BOLIVIA
La Paz
Arequipa

Lake Poopo
Sucre

B R A Z I L

Mato Grosso plateau

Brasilia
Goiania

Brazilian Highlands

Salvador

Belo Horizonte

Atacama Desert

Chaco

Gran

PARAGUAY

Parana

Sao Paulo

Rio de Janeiro
Tropic of Capricorn

C H I L E

ARGENTINA

Curitiba

Porto Alegre

South America inset map
ATLANTIC OCEAN

Equator

Height of the land
▲ Highest point on the map

over 6000 metres
4000 - 6000
2000 - 4000
1000 - 2000
400 - 1000
200 - 400
0 - 200 metres
below sea level
sea level

■●● Country boundaries
Large cities
Lima Capital cities underlined

Scale 1:30 000 000
0 300km 600km 900km 1200km 1500km
1 cm on the map = 300 km on the ground
0 300miles 600miles 900miles
1 inch on the map = 480 miles on the ground

West from Greenwich 80°
© COPYRIGHT. GEORGE PHILIP & SON. LTD.

Cattle and cowboys. *To the south of the Amazon jungle, there is a large area of dry woodland and grassland in Brazil called the Mato Grosso. Cattle are grazed here, and horses are still used to round them up.*

Did you know?

Ecuador means *Equator*: the Equator (0°) crosses the country.
Colombia is named after Christopher *Columbus*, who sailed from Europe to the Americas in 1492.

Bolivia is named after Simon *Bolivar*, a hero of the country's war of independence in the 1820s.
La Paz, the biggest town in Bolivia, means *peace*. But there have been over 100 revolutions in Bolivia, the highest total in the world!

TEMPERATE SOUTH AMERICA

Chile is 4300 kilometres long, but only about 200 kilometres wide, because it is sandwiched between the Andes and the Pacific. In the *north* is the Atacama desert, the driest in the world. In one place, there was no rain for 400 years! Fortunately, rivers from the Andes permit some irrigation. Chilean nitrates come from this area. Nitrates are salts in dried-up lakes; they are used to make fertilizers and explosives.

In the *centre*, the climate is like the Mediterranean area and California, with hot dry summers and warm wet winters with westerly winds (six words begin with W: it's easy to remember!) This is a lovely climate, and most Chileans live in this area.

In the *south*, Chile is wet, windy and cool. Thick forests which include the Chilean pine (monkey-puzzle tree) cover the steep hills. The reason for these contrasts is the wind. Winds bringing cloud and rain blow from the Pacific Ocean all year in the south; but only in winter in the centre; and not at all in the north.

▲ **Geysers in the Andes, Chile.** *Hot steam hisses into the cold air, 4000 metres above sea-level in the Andes of northern Chile.*

The Falkland Islands

These islands are a British colony in the South Atlantic. They are about 480 kilometres east of Argentina, which claims them as the Islas Malvinas. Britain fought an Argentine invasion in 1982, and the military force is now as large as the population (only 2000). Sheep-farming is the main occupation.

The capital city, Port Stanley, has houses that look quite like English houses, but the remote farmhouses get their post by 'mail drop' from a Beaver aircraft (see stamp above). Until recently, there were no roads to these farms. This stamp shows Argentina's claim that the Falkland Islands are part of Argentina.

The Andes

The Andes are over 7000 kilometres long, so they are the longest mountain range in the world. They are fold mountains, with a very steep western side, and a gentler eastern side. Most of the high peaks are volcanoes: they are the highest volcanoes in the world. Mount Aconcagua (6960 metres) is an extinct volcano. Mount Guallatiri, in Chile, is the world's highest active volcano – it last erupted in 1969.

The higher you climb, the cooler it is. And the further you travel from the Equator, the cooler it is. Therefore, the snowline in southern Chile is *much* lower than in northern Chile.

Argentina means 'silvery' in Spanish: some of the early settlers came to mine silver. But today, Argentina's most important product is cattle. Cool grasslands called the Pampas are ideal for cattle-grazing.

Argentina is a varied country: the northwest is hot and dry, and the south is cold and dry (see photograph). The frontier with Chile runs high along the top of the Andes.

Buenos Aires, the capital city, is the biggest city in South America; it has 10 million people. The name means 'good air', but petrol fumes have now polluted the air.

Paraguay and **Uruguay** are two countries with small populations. Each country has about three million people. Nearly half the population of Uruguay lives in the capital city, Montevideo, which is on the coast. In contrast Paraguay is completely landlocked. Animal-farming is the most important occupation in both these countries.

Sheep farming in Patagonia, Argentina. *Southern Argentina has a cool, dry climate. Very few people live there – but lots of sheep roam the extensive grasslands. There are more sheep than people in Argentina: 45 million sheep, but only 30 million people!*

THE PACIFIC

This map shows half the world. Guess which place is furthest from a continent: it is somewhere in the south Pacific. The Pacific also includes the deepest place in the world: the Mariana Trench (11,022 metres deep). It would take over an hour for a steel ball weighing half a kilogram to fall to the bottom!

There are thousands of islands in the Pacific Ocean. Some are volcanic mountains, while many others are low, flat coral islands. Coral also grows round the volcanoes (see photograph below).

A few islands have valuable minerals – for example Nauru (phosphates) and Bougainville (copper). But most islanders are occupied in farming. Many tropical crops grow well; sugarcane, bananas and pineapple are important exports. Islands big enough for a full-sized airport, such as Fiji, the Samoan islands, Tahiti, and Hawaii (see page 66), now get many globe-trotting tourists.

Moorea from the air. *The coral reef can be clearly seen around this island in French Polynesia; the reef makes it difficult for ships to reach the land.*

The island is steep and rugged: it is an old volcano. Notice the deep valleys dug by rivers. The white patches are clouds, not snow.

▼

Easter Island, South Pacific. *These huge stone sculptures each weigh about 50 tonnes! They were cut long ago with simple stone axes, and lifted with ropes and ramps – an amazing achievement for people who had no metal, no wheels and no machines.*

Look for Easter Island on the map (in square U 11): it is one of the remotest places in the world. It is now owned by Chile, 3860 kilometres away in South America.

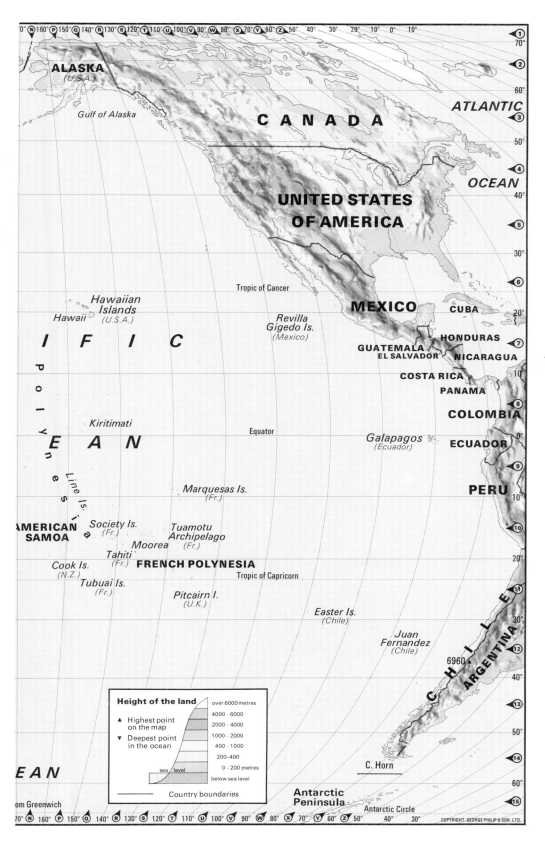

Most Pacific countries are large groups of small islands. Their boundaries are out at sea – just lines on a map. Kiribati is 33 small coral atolls spread over 5 million square kilometres of ocean. And the Solomon Islands stretch for 1450 kilometres. Imagine organizing something for the whole country!

Pacific stamps

The stamp from **French Polynesia** shows coconut-palms – and an outrigger canoe: you can see how this makes the dug-out canoe more stable at sea. In the background, there are canoes with sails.

In the highlands of **Papua New Guinea** (north of Australia), people live in round huts with thatched roofs. The stamp also shows the island's high, rugged mountains.

AUSTRALIA

PAPUA NEW GUINEA

INDONESIA

Arafura   Sea

Torres Strait

C. York

Timor

Melville I.

C. Arnhem

Weipa

Sea

Darwin

Arnhem

Cape

Gulf of

York

Land

Carpentaria

Peninsula

INDIAN

Wyndham

NORTHERN

Cairns

Coral

Kimberley

Cairns

Sea

OCEAN

Broome

Fitzroy

Tanami

Desert

Great Barrier Reef

Townsville

Great Sandy

Mount Isa

QUEENSLAND

Desert

TERRITORY

Dampier

Macdonnell

Tropic of Capricorn

Hamersley

Ranges

Alice Springs

Barcoo

Range

Mount

Rockhampton

Newman

Gibson Desert

△ Ayers Rock

Bundaberg

WESTERN

Musgrave Ranges

Warrego

Charleville

SOUTH

L. Eyre

Brisbane

Great Victoria

Toowoomba

AUSTRALIA *Desert*

AUSTRALIA

Geraldton

L. Torrens

Darling

Kalgoorlie-

L.

NEW   SOUTH

Boulder

Gairdner

Broken

Hill

Lachlan

Blue

Perth

Nullarbor Plain

Whyalla

Port Pirie

WALES

Mountains

Newcastle

Whyalla

Murray

Murrumbidgee

Sydney

Great Australian Bight

Adelaide

Wollongong

Cape Leeuwin

Kangaroo I.

Canberra

Albany

VICTORIA Mt. Kosciusko

△ 2230

Australian

Alps

Geelong

Melbourne

SOUTHERN   OCEAN

Bass Strait

TASMANIA

Launceston

Hobart

Height of the land

over 6000 metres
4000 - 6000
2000 - 4000
1000 - 2000
400 - 1000
200 - 400
0 - 200 metres
below sea level

▲ Highest point on the map

sea level

Country boundaries
Large cities
Canberra Capital city underlined

Scale 1:20 000 000

0   200km   400km   600km   800km   1000km   1200km

1 cm on the map = 200 km on the ground

0   200miles   400miles   600miles   800miles

1 inch on the map = 320 miles on the ground

84

The Indian-Pacific Express

Town	Time	Day no.	Distance (kilometres)
Perth	21.00	1	0
Kalgoorlie	07.00	2	657
Port Pirie	14.00	3	2439
Broken Hill	20.54	3	2836
Sydney	15.55	4	3961

It takes three nights and three days to cross Australia by train, from Perth to Sydney. The map shows you why the train is called the Indian-Pacific.

Australia is the world's largest island, but the smallest continent. It is the sixth-largest country in the world, smaller than the USA or Canada, but more than twice the size of India. Yet Australia has only about 15 million people. Most Australians are descended from people who came from Europe in the past 150 years.

The map shows that all the state capitals are on the coast, but Canberra, the national capital, is inland. Most Australians live in towns near the coast.

Only a few people live in the mountains or in the outback – the enormous area of semi-desert and desert that makes up most of the country. The few outback people live on huge sheep and cattle farms, in mining-towns, or on special reserves for the original Australians, the Aborigines. Yet the wool, the meat, and the minerals of the outback are important exports.

The Great Barrier Reef *is the world's largest living thing! It is an area of coral over 2000 kilometres long, which grows in the warm sea near the coast of Queensland.*

Ayers Rock *is in the heart of the desert in central Australia. Nothing grows on its steep sides. At sunset, it looks bright red!*

Christmas 'down under' *is in midsummer. Justine's stamp shows a typical Australian Christmas at the seaside, with swimming and sunbathing. But she didn't forget Father Christmas, with his red coat and his reindeer!*

Animals in Australia. *Australia is not joined to any other continent. It has been a separate island for millions of years, and has developed its own unique wildlife.*

The first stamps for the whole of Australia showed the country's most famous animal (far right). The kangaroo is a marsupial, which means 'pouched' – mother has her

own 'pocket' for baby Roo! Most of the world's marsupials live in Australia. Four of these animals are endangered species: they will die out unless they are protected.

NEW ZEALAND

The Antipodes

New Zealand is on the opposite side of the Earth from Europe. This double map shows that the far north of New Zealand is at the same latitude as North Africa, and that the far south of New Zealand is at the same latitude as Paris.

The New Zealand flag includes the British flag, because it was a British colony for over 150 years. Most New Zealand families originally came from Britain. The stars are known as the Southern Cross.

The two main islands that make up New Zealand are 2000 kilometres east of Australia. Only 3½ million people live in the whole country. The capital is Wellington, near the centre of New Zealand, but the largest city is Auckland in the north.

The original inhabitants were the Maoris, but now they are only about 8 per cent of the population. Some place-names are Maori words, such as Rotorua and Wanganui.

South Island is the largest island, but has fewer people than North Island. There are far more sheep than people! Mount Cook, the highest point in New Zealand (3764 metres), is in the spectacular Southern Alps. Tourists visit the far south to see the glaciers and fjords. The fast-flowing rivers are used for hydro-electricity.

A geothermal power-station *in North Island. In this volcanic area there is natural hot steam underground which can be piped to power-stations to produce electricity.*

▼

North Island has a warmer climate than South Island. In some places you can see hot springs and boiling mud pools and there are also volcanoes. Fine trees and giant ferns grow in the forests, but much of the forest has been cleared for farming. Cattle are kept on the rich grasslands for meat and milk. Many different kinds of fruit grow well, including apples and kiwi-fruit.

New Zealand exports

These stamps show some major exports: pine trees become sawn timber for export (10c); sheep's wool is spun for export (18c); the 20 cent stamp shows cattle hides and skins being lifted onto a ship; while the 25 cent stamp shows cartons of New Zealand butter being loaded. Notice the snow-covered volcanic mountain in the background.

Sheep grazing on the Canterbury Plains, *in South Island. New Zealand lamb is exported to Europe and North America in refrigerated ships. In the distance are the snow-covered Southern Alps. This great mountain range has glaciers, fjords and ski-slopes.*

▼

ANTARCTIC

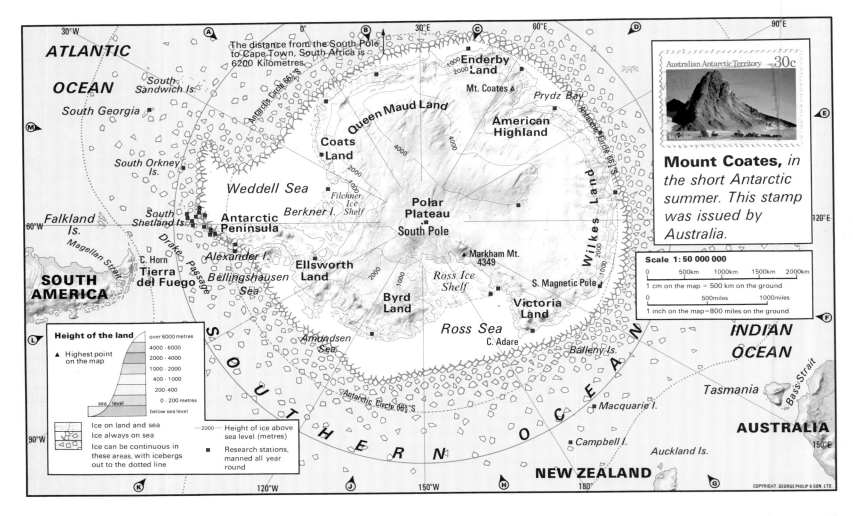

The distance from the South Pole to Cape Town, South Africa is 6200 Kilometres

ATLANTIC OCEAN

South Sandwich Is.

South Georgia

South Orkney Is.

Weddell Sea

Falkland Is.

Magellan Strait

C. Horn

SOUTH AMERICA

Tierra del Fuego

South Shetland Is.

Antarctic Peninsula

Alexander I.

Bellingshausen Sea

Drake Passage

Enderby Land

Queen Maud Land

Coats Land

Mt. Coates

Prydz Bay

American Highland

Berkner I.

Filchner Ice Shelf

Polar Plateau

South Pole

Markham Mt. 4349

Ross Ice Shelf

S. Magnetic Pole

Wilkes Land

Ellsworth Land

Byrd Land

Victoria Land

Ross Sea

C. Adare

Amundsen Sea

Balleny Is.

INDIAN OCEAN

Tasmania

Bass Strait

AUSTRALIA

Macquarie I.

Campbell I.

Auckland Is.

NEW ZEALAND

SOUTHERN OCEAN

Antarctic Circle 66½°S

Height of the land

over 6000 metres
4000 - 6000
2000 - 4000
1000 - 2000
400 - 1000
200 - 400
0 - 200 metres
below sea level

▲ Highest point on the map

sea level

Ice on land and sea
Ice always on sea

Ice can be continuous in these areas, with icebergs out to the dotted line

—2000— Height of ice above sea level (metres)

■ Research stations, manned all year round

Mount Coates, *in the short Antarctic summer. This stamp was issued by Australia.*

Australian Antarctic Territory 30c

Scale 1:50 000 000

0   500km   1000km   1500km   2000km
1 cm on the map = 500 km on the ground
0   500miles   1000miles
1 inch on the map = 800 miles on the ground

COPYRIGHT. GEORGE PHILIP & SON. LTD.

Emperor penguins *with chicks. Penguins cannot fly, but they can swim very well. The parents use their feet to protect the eggs and chicks from the cold ice! No land animals live in Antarctica, but the ocean is full of fish, which provide food for penguins, seals and whales.*
▼

Fact box: Antarctica

5th largest continent – about 13,900,000 square kilometres

Surrounded by cold **seas**
South Pole **first reached** in 1911

Antarctica is the continent surrounding the South Pole. It is the coldest, windiest and iciest place in the world! It is also very isolated, as the map shows.

No people live in Antarctica permanently. Some scientists work in research stations.

Everything that is needed in Antarctica has to be brought in during the short summer. From November to January, icebreakers can reach the land. But huge icebergs are always a danger. In winter (May to July) it is always dark, the sea is frozen, and people have to face extreme cold and dangerous blizzards.

ARCTIC

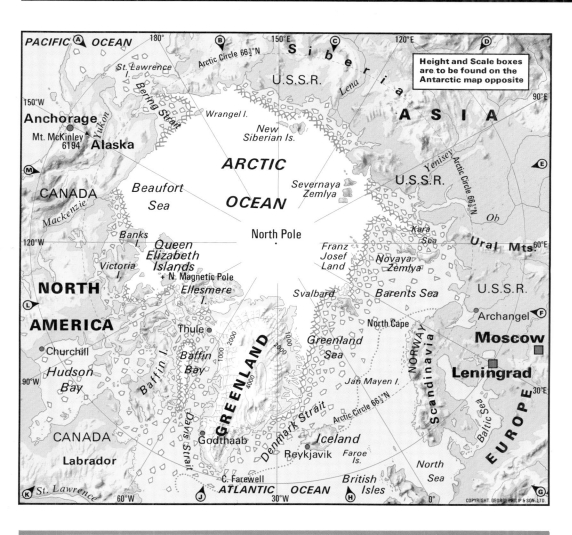

The Arctic is an ocean, which is frozen throughout the winter. It is surrounded by the northernmost areas of three continents, but Greenland is the only truly Arctic country.

For most of the year the land is snow-covered. During the short summer, when the sun never sets, the snow and the frozen topsoil melt. But the deeper soil is still frozen, so the land is very marshy. This treeless landscape is called the tundra.

The reindeer and caribou can be herded or hunted, but farming is impossible. In recent years, rich mineral deposits have been found. Canada, the USA and USSR have military bases facing each other across the Arctic Ocean.

Eskimos. *The Inuit (Eskimos) have lived in the Arctic for thousands of years by hunting and fishing. These men (left) are resting their husky dogs which are trained to pull sledges.*

The Inuit only build igloos as emergency shelters. Most of them live in wooden buildings that are well insulated against the cold, like the Greenland family (above), and most are more likely to travel by motorized skidoo than by sledge. Many work in mining camps, military bases and weather stations.

Fact box: Arctic

4th largest ocean – about 14,000,000 square kilometres

World record for least sunshine and tallest iceberg
Surrounded by cold **land**
North Pole **first reached** in 1909

QUIZ

Name the island

The name of the continent where each island is found is marked on each outline. Do you know (*a*) the name of each island and (*b*) to which country each island belongs (or are they island countries)?

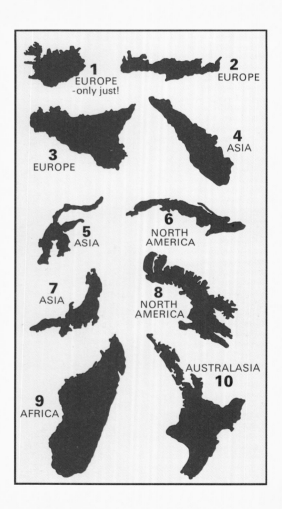

Name the country

There is a long, thin country in almost every continent. Can you name the countries shown here – and name the continent in which they are found? (If you need help, look at pages 8–9 for a map of the countries of the world.)

A mystery message

Use the map of the countries of the world on pages 8–9 to decode this message. Each missing word is all or part of the name of a country. (For some answers, letters have to be taken out of or added to the name of the country.)

I was _____ (east of Austria), so I bought a large _____ (east of Greece), some _____ns (east of Norway) and a bottle of _____ (west of Spain). Finally, I ate an ___land (west of Norway) -cream. I enjoyed my _e__ (east of Mauritania), but afterwards I began to _____ea__a (south of Romania) and I got a bad $____ (south of France). A Ø___ (east of Saudi Arabia) told me: 'Just eat Philip_____apples (south of Taiwan) and __gypt (east of Libya), cooked in a Ja___ (east of Korea). Tomorrow you can eat a Cuban___ (east of Ivory Coast) and some _____ (east of Peru) nuts. It shouldn't _____a Rica (west of Panama) you too much.' I said: 'You must be ___agascar (east of Mozambique)! I think I've got ____ysr__ (north of Indonesia). I'll have __/__ (west of Benin) to a doctor quickly, otherwise I'll soon be ____ Sea (lake between Israel and Jordan).' Happily, the doctor __bared (island country south of USA) me, so I am still M__d___s (islands west of Sri Lanka) today!

Oceans and seas

What ocean would you cross on an aeroplane journey. . .
1 From Australia to the USA?
2 From Brazil to South Africa?
3 From Canada to the USSR?
4 From Madagascar to Indonesia?
90 5 From Mexico to Portugal?

What sea would you cross on an aeroplane journey. . .
6 From Saudi Arabia to Egypt?
7 From Korea to Japan?
8 From Denmark to the United Kingdom?
9 From Vietnam to the Philippines?
10 From Cuba to Colombia?

Places in Asia

Move the letters to find:

Countries
RAIN; CHAIN; MOAN; AWAIT N.
Capital cities
DEAN; I HELD; A BULK; KEG NIP; LOUSE; DIARY H.

Find the colour

Each answer is a colour. Use the atlas index and the maps to help you.

Cover the right-hand column with a piece of paper and try to answer the left-hand column only. Award yourself *2* points for each correct answer to the left-hand column only, or *1* point if you used the clues in both columns.

1 A sea between Egypt and Saudi Arabia. . .

2 A huge island east of Canada. . .

3 The sea between Turkey and the USSR. . .

4 The sea between Korea and China. . .

5 The sea on which Archangel lies, in the USSR. . .

6 A town in southern France which is also a fruit. . .

7 The tributary of the River Nile that flows from Ethiopia to Khartoum (Sudan). . .

. . .and the river on the border of Oklahoma and Texas, USA.

. . .and a bay on the west side of Lake Michigan, USA.

. . .and a forest in Germany.

. . .and a (stony?) river in Wyoming, USA.

. . .and the river flowing north from Lake Victoria to Khartoum (Sudan).

. . .and the river which makes the border between South Africa and Namibia.

. . .and a mountain ridge in eastern USA.

How well do you know the states of the USA?

All the answers can be found on the maps on pages 62–3 and 66–9. Do not include Alaska and Hawaii.

1 Which is the *biggest* state?
2 Which is the *smallest* state?
3 Which state reaches furthest *north*? (careful!)
4 Which state reaches furthest *south*?
5 Which state reaches furthest *west*?
6 Which state reaches furthest *east*?
7 Which state is split into two by a lake?
8 Which state is split into two by an inlet of the sea?
9 Which two states are perfect rectangles in shape?
10 Which state is shaped like a saucepan?
11 In which state would you be if you visited Lake Huron?
12 In which state would you be if you visited Lake Ontario?
13 In which state would you be if you visited the Great Salt Lake?
14 In which state would you be if you visited the Mississippi delta?

15 Which state in *northern* USA is called South   ?
16 Which state in *southern* USA is called North   ?
17 There is only one place in the USA where four states meet: which states?
18 How many states have a border with Mexico?
19 How many states have a coastline on the Pacific?
20 How many states have a coastline on the Gulf of Mexico?

Great rivers of Europe

Use pages 18–39 to discover which great river flows through or near each pair of towns or cities.
1 Vienna, Austria and Budapest, Hungary.
2 Rotterdam, Netherlands and Bonn, West Germany.
3 Avignon, France and Lyons, France.
4 Worcester, England and Gloucester, England.
5 Toledo, Spain and Lisbon, Portugal.

Things To Do

Where do the things you use come from?

What do you and your family use, eat or wear from different countries of the world? In this atlas you will find lists of some items we have found (pages 27 and 37). Now you can do some spotting.

Collect stamps with a theme

A stamp collection soon grows. Try a *thematic* collection: choose a theme (topic) and collect stamps on that theme. For example, you could collect: *Flags* on stamps. Togo had a flag stamp for Independence Day.

Map stamps: small islands often issue map stamps to show everyone where they are!

Traditional crafts on stamps: this Zambian thatcher is using a home-made ladder.

Make your own coin collection

Ask people who have been abroad for any foreign coins they do not want – you will have an instant collection! If you cannot have the coins to keep, you could make pencil or crayon rubbings on thin paper. Look at the pictures of coins in the atlas. Look at your coins for examples of languages; crops; famous buildings; historic events. . . .

INDEX

How to Use this Index

The first number given after each name or topic is the page number; then a letter and another number tell you which square of the map you should look at.

For example, Abidjan is in square B2 on page 56. Find B at the top or bottom of the map on page 56 and put a finger on it. Put another finger on the number 2 at the side of the map. Move your fingers in from the edge of the map and they will meet in square B2. Abidjan will now be easy to find. It is the capital city of the Ivory Coast, a country in West Africa.

If a name goes through more than one square, the square given in the index is the one in which the biggest part of the name falls.
Names like *Gulf of Mexico* and *Cape Horn* are in the Index index as *Mexico, Gulf of* and *Horn, Cape.*

ANSWERS TO QUESTIONS

Answers to text questions

page 18 Western Europe's most important building: the Headquarters of the European Community in Brussels, the capital of Belgium. In this building many of the important decisions about Western Europe are made. The photograph shows reflections in the double-glazed windows. In the reflection you can see small old houses and shops and big modern office buildings in Brussels, the biggest city in Belgium.

page 19 B = Belgium; D = West Germany (Deutschland in German); DK = Denmark; E = Spain (España); F = France; GB = Great Britain; GR = Greece; I = Italy; IRL = Ireland (Republic of Ireland); L = Luxembourg; NL = Netherlands; P = Portugal.

page 21 The London landmarks featured on the stamp are (*left to right*): Westminster Abbey; Nelson's column (in Trafalgar Square); statue of Eros in Piccadilly Circus; Telecom Tower; clock tower of the Houses of Parliament (containing the bell Big Ben); St Paul's Cathedral; Tower Bridge; White Tower of the Tower of London.

page 25 Belgium has two official languages, French and Flemish. The coin on the left has the French name for Belgium, that on the right its Flemish name.

page 27 The vegetables on the stall are green and red peppers, aubergines, onions and tomatoes, with some cucumbers and baby marrows on the left.

page 29 The international clock in East Berlin: the names on the clock stay still; the numbers move slowly round. In 24 hours, the numbers have turned a full circle – just like the Earth in space! When the photograph was taken, at 16.00 hours (4 pm) in Berlin, it was 13.30 hours (1.30 pm) in Reykjavik, Iceland, and 17.00 hours (5 pm) in Helsinki, Finland. In places *west* of Berlin it is earlier in the day; in places *east* of Berlin, it is later in the day. Note the names on the clock are in German.

page 37 The flags on the stamp show the Warsaw Pact countries: (*top row, left to right*) Bulgaria, Cuba (in West Indies), Romania; (*centre row, left to right*) Hungary, Mongolia (in Asia), USSR; (*bottom row, left to right*) East Germany (German Democratic Republic), Poland, Czechoslovakia.

page 55 Puzzle picture: the circles are 'drawn' by huge centre-pivot irrigation sprays, which turn slowly to make the shape of a circle. Each circle is about 1 kilometre across. The irrigation allows crops to grow in the desert. Some of the crops in the circular 'fields' are already ripening, so they look less green.

page 57 Puzzle picture: this farmer in Ghana is making a mound of earth over each yam tuber he has planted.

page 62 The photograph of the fruit market shows (*at back*) bananas, pineapple; (*centre*) breadfruit, mango, lime; (*at front*) grapefruit, lemons, pawpaw, pineapple. There are vegetables on display behind.

page 63 The north shores of Lakes Superior, Huron, Erie and Ontario are in Canada, and the south shores in the USA. Lake Michigan is entirely in the USA.

page 63 El Salvador only has a coastline on the Pacific Ocean.

Belize only has a coastline on the Caribbean Sea. (Honduras has a tiny coastline on the Pacific – look closely at the map!)

page 67 Seattle to Miami is 5445 kilometres; New Orleans to Chicago is 1488 kilometres.

page 69 The stamp shows the Mississippi river. It flows southwards to New Orleans and the Gulf of Mexico. It was used for transport far into the heart of America long before roads were built, so it became known as the 'Great River Road'.

Answers to quiz

Name the island
(Name of country in brackets after name of island)
1 Iceland (Iceland); 2 Crete (Greece); 3 Sicily (Italy); 4 Sumatra (Indonesia); 5 Sulawesi (Indonesia); 6 Cuba (Cuba); 7 Honshu (Japan); 8 Baffin Island (Canada); 9 Madagascar (Madagascar); 10 North Island (New Zealand)

Name the country
(Name of continent in brackets after name of country)
1 Norway (Europe); 2 Thailand (Asia); 3 Mozambique (Africa); 4 Mexico (Central America); 5 Chile (South America).

Oceans and seas
1 Pacific; 2 Atlantic; 3 Arctic; 4 Indian; 5 Atlantic; 6 Red Sea; 7 Sea of Japan; 8 North Sea; 9 South China Sea; 10 Caribbean Sea.

A mystery message
I was *hungry*, so I bought a large *turkey*, some *swedes* and a bottle of *port*. Finally, I ate an *ice*-cream. I enjoyed my *meal*, but afterwards I began to *bulge* and I got a bad *pain*. A *man* told me: 'Just eat *pineapples* and *egg* cooked in a *pan*. Tomorrow you can eat a *banana* and some *Brazil* nuts. It shouldn't *cost* you too much.' I said: 'You must be *mad*! I think I've got *malaria*. I'll have *to go* to a doctor quickly, otherwise I'll soon be *dead*.'

Happily, the doctor *cured* me, so I am still *alive* today!

Places in Asia
Countries Iran; China; Oman; Taiwan.
Capital cities Aden; Delhi; Kabul; Peking; Seoul; Riyadh.

Colour quiz
1 Red (Red Sea/Red River); 2 Green (Greenland/Green Bay); 3 Black (Black Sea/Black Forest); 4 Yellow (Yellow Sea/Yellowstone River); 5 White (White Sea/White Nile); 6 Orange (Orange/Orange River); 7 Blue (Blue Nile/Blue Ridge, USA).

Score
13–14 Brilliant! 10–12 Very well done. 6–9 Good. 2–5 Use this atlas more – you'll soon do better. 0–1 Try another planet – there's less geography there.

States of the USA
1 Texas;   2 Rhode Island; 3 Minnesota;   4 Florida; 5 California;   6 Maine; 7 Michigan;   8 Maryland; 9 Wyoming and Colorado; 10 Oklahoma;   11 Michigan; 12 New York;   13 Utah; 14 Louisiana;   15 South Dakota; 16 North Carolina;   17 Utah, Colorado, Arizona and New Mexico;   18 Four;   19 Three; 20 Five.

Great rivers of Europe
1 Danube; 2 Rhine; 3 Rhône; 4 Severn; 5 Tagus.

Illustration Acknowledgements
The Australian Tourist Commission p. 85 (top); *Bruce Coleman Limited* p. 6, p. 8, p. 11 (right), p. 15 (left), p. 21 (below right), p. 23 (above right), p. 27 (top), p. 29 (below left), p. 32 (below), p. 37 (top), p. 39 (below), p. 40, p. 54 (top), p. 59, p. 61 (right), p. 69 (above left), p. 70 (top left and below), p. 72 (top), p. 78 (top), p. 80 (below), p. 82, p. 83, p. 87, p. 89

(below); *The Daily Telegraph* p. 5; *Susan Griggs* p. 11 (left), p. 21 (top), p. 23 (below right), p. 31 (top), p. 33, p. 38, p. 39 (top), p. 42 (right), p. 43 (top), p. 45 (below), p. 50 (above left), p. 62, p. 63, p. 65 (right), p. 67, p. 70 (top right), p. 72 (below), p. 73, p. 76; *Robert Harding Picture Library* p. 15 (right), p. 19, p. 41, p. 45 (centre), p. 47 (top), p. 49 (centre and below left),

p. 50 (below), p. 58 (below left), p. 61 (left), p. 64 (left), p. 75 (top left), p. 78 (below left), p. 88; *The J. Allan Cash Photolibrary* p. 12, p. 25 (below right), p. 29 (right), p. 31 (below left), p. 45 (top), p. 48, p. 50 (above right), p. 54 (below left), p. 56, p. 57 (top left), p. 58 (top and below right), p. 75 (below), p. 78 (below right); *NASA* title page, p. 55 (below left); *The Quentin Bell*

Organisation p. 64 (right); *Ralph Somerville* p. 49 (top); *Spanish National Tourist Office* p. 31 (centre); *Vautier-de-Nanxe* p. 42 (left), p. 71, p. 77, p. 80 (top), p. 81; *David and Jill Wright* p. 10, p. 14, p. 16, p. 18, p. 21 (below right), p. 22, p. 23 (below left), p. 25 (top and below left), p. 27 (centre and below), p. 29 (top), p. 31 (below right), p. 34 (left), p. 35, p. 43

(below), p. 44, p. 47 (below left), p. 52, p. 54 (below right), p. 57 (top right, centre and below), p. 60, p. 68 (above), p. 69 (centre and top left), p. 75 (top right), p. 85 (centre); *Zefa* p. 11 (centre), p. 20, p. 23 (above left), p. 24, p. 28, p. 32 (top), p. 34 (right), p. 37 (below, right and left), p. 53, p. 55 (below right), p. 65 (left), p. 68 (below), p. 79, p. 89 (centre).